# WALKING

# WITH HIM

# WALKING

## 52 DEVOTIONS THROUGH *LUKE* AND *ACTS*

# WITH HIM

## BY JAMES A. LITTLES JR.

WORD AFLAME PRESS
WELDON SPRING, MO

Word Aflame Press
36 Research Park Court
Weldon Spring, MO 63304
pentecostalpublishing.com

Cover design by Jeremy Hart

Printed in the United States of America

32 31 30 29 28 27 26 25 24 23      1 2 3 4 5

---

Library of Congress Cataloging-in-Publication Data

Names: Littles, James A., Jr., 1961- author.
Title: Walking with him : Fifty-two devotions through Luke and Acts / by James A. Littles, Jr.
Description: Weldon Spring, MO : Word Aflame Press, [2023] | Summary: "This book chronicles the author's reading of the Gospel of Luke and the Book of Acts and a chapter-by-chapter application of the text to his life"-- Provided by publisher.
Identifiers: LCCN 2023009943 (print) | LCCN 2023009944 (ebook) | ISBN 9780757760310 (paperback) | ISBN 9780757760327 (epub)
Subjects: LCSH: Bible. Luke--Meditations. | Bible. Acts--Meditations. | Christian life--Meditations.
Classification: LCC BS2589 .L585 2023 (print) | LCC BS2589 (ebook) | DDC 226.4/06--dc23/eng/20230518
LC record available at https://lccn.loc.gov/2023009943
LC ebook record available at https://lccn.loc.gov/2023009944

*I dedicate this book to my wife and special best friend, Sherri Lynn Daniels Littles.*

*She and I have had the privilege of walking together since 1980.*

*We began the journey with assurance of God's goodness and claim on our lives. Now over the decades we have confirmed God is indeed faithful to those who follow Him.*

# Contents

# Preface

They that wait upon the Lord shall renew their strength; they shall mount up with wings as eagles; they shall run, and not be weary; and they shall walk, and not faint. (Isaiah 40:31)

The frenetic contemporary world lives by aphorisms such as "time is money." Most people think they do not have enough of either one. Many citizens of the western world live harried lives where the default daily goal is just to make it to the end of the week. Following Jesus calls for a radically different view of life.

Jesus taught His followers that bigger barns are not always better, outcasts deserve to be valued and respected, and occasionally caring for a man in the ditch should have priority over getting to worship service on time. Jesus' followers had to learn a new life rhythm. And they learned it by following the Teacher together. They did not graduate from Jesus' discipleship program by measuring time—they had to learn the Father was in control of the seasons and the times. Getting the Father's attention did not result from lengthy prayers or loudness of intercessions any more than it did for the ancient prophet Elijah.

I wrote most of these devotions by posting my reflection journal entries on Facebook rather than on nice cotton paper that I usually use. The process held me accountable to continue in my commitment to seek "first the kingdom of God, and his righteousness." I wanted to intentionally practice a life surrendered to Jesus' promise that "all these things shall be added unto you" (Matthew 6:33). The devotional method came from Jesus' teaching in John 15. The Father answers prayers for those who abide in Jesus while they have His word abiding in them.

My original context for writing the early entries included many social changes such as ministry shifts and moving to a different state. Some of the later entries happened after the passing of both of my parents. Times of crises often cause people to regress to a prior level of functioning. While this happened at many points of the journey in my daily thoughts and spiritual questions, my devotions stayed committed to following Jesus through Luke and Acts and praying the Word rather than defaulting to my old strategy of listing my needs and wants. I chose Luke and Acts because I believe the gospel writer was writing volume one and two of a unified work that demonstrated Jesus coming into the world, His journeying toward Jerusalem's cross, commissioning His disciples to continue His same incarnational ministry to go into all the world with the Spirit's empowerment.

I wanted to follow Jesus with those disciples. I wanted those words to be embedded in me. Each chapter's reflection typically took two to four days to complete. I would soak myself in the chapter for as long as it took to lay down my morning worries and hear the Word above every other voice. Pastoral theologian Ed Wimberly calls this privileging God's conversation. I needed to make sure that voice set my trajectory rather than any circumstances or emotions I might experience. After hanging out in the Word for a while I was ready to write. Each entry began with some type of human-interest event, song, or personal experience of growing up in a church planter's home with three brothers. Those opening remarks took me from my world into the world narrated by Luke.

I followed Jesus.

Readers looking for biblical exegesis will be disappointed. I value the work of my exegetical brothers and sisters, but these devotions caused me to dive into the Word and let the Word dissect my life. I wanted to be transformed like the fishermen and tax collectors who left boat and table to follow their Rabbi.

I followed Jesus.

Immersion in Jesus' journey usually ended in a repentance prayer. I find I rarely see Jesus' hem filling the temple surrounded by angels enunciating His holy attributes. I do not think it happened one time, yet encountering Jesus on the road repeatedly called me to repentance as it did Isaiah. Repentance led to a variety of prayers and intercessions that flowed from the experience with Jesus rather than the pain of boxing possessions, selling a home, and trying to adapt to a different ministry framework. I wanted answered prayers . . . the kind that only come from following Jesus and letting His words impregnate my spirit.

Many of my Facebook friends encouraged me to finish the project and put them into a book. This devotional is a result of those loving provocations. In return, I am asking the reader to follow a similar process. I think the most beneficial use of this devotional will look something like this:

- Pray for God to open your mind, heart, actions, and relationships as you follow Jesus through Luke and Acts.

- Read the chapter through multiple times. Go more slowly with each read through as the interferences around you lose their power and the Word becomes the most prominent voice in your life.

- Think on the chapter all during the day.

- On the second day reread the chapter again to reset its stamp on your mind and spirit.

- Read my devotional reflections so we can follow Jesus together. Make the Word your prayer agenda as you read my prayer and begin praying your own insights from the chapter.

- On the third day reread the chapter from Luke or Acts, and then write out your own response to the chapter. Celebrate moments of transformation. Lament moments when noises around you cause you to fall behind the Teacher's leading. Rest in knowing Jesus is doing the work to make you more like Him as you serve on His mission.

- Where possible, find ways to share your ideas with others. Following Jesus almost always includes becoming more vulnerable with fellow travelers.

Of course, if a different rhythm works for you, then use the book in a way that is most beneficial to you. You will probably finish the Luke-Acts itinerary in a shorter period of time than I did, but we are still walking the road together. I may have the opportunity to meet some of you fellow travelers in this life. I look forward to hearing how the Teacher is making you more like Him in the journey. The other anticipated meeting will happen when our journeys transition from this world to the next. We will truly be different then because we will see Him as He really is.

Thank you for following Jesus with me.

Jim

# 1 | A *WALK* THROUGH LUKE 1

I am not really a bucket list kind of guy. Given my personality, I am afraid the list would turn into something to chase—another work item to accomplish. Instead I have had some lifetime experiences to celebrate and remember. Some lifetime experiences are trips such as the ones my wife, Sherri, and I got to take to Whitehorse, Yukon, and to Singapore. Just mentioning those trips brings memories of shared meals with dear friends, fishing trips, preaching and teaching in special places, and walks with my princess. Another lifetime experience expanded to fill my middle adult years—who would have thought I would have the opportunity to be a Bible college instructor for eleven years and seminary professor for seventeen more years? Now that Sherri and I live quite a distance from all of our family members, each visit gives me a chance for double hugs with my parents, children, grandchildren, brothers, and other family members. Those moments provide a deeper joy and pleasure than the trips to Austria and Switzerland that I have recently daydreamed about ever could.

Kissing Sherri's shoulder as I left for the office this morning was a lifetime experience. I've done it a thousand times or more over the last thirty-nine years, but each one is a once-in-a-lifetime experience.

Some "bucket-listable" experiences do not live up to the anticipation. I've had a few such honors and experiences, but

I will leave them unnamed. I do not want to taint someone else's anticipation or memories of those times.

Reflecting on these past blessings changes me. They turn me from disappointments, losses, and grief to anticipation, thanksgiving, and hope. The Lord's blessings come as gifts rather than payments for my efforts or "sacrifice." Blessings remind me that sacrifice draws from an understanding of worship rather than a part of economic theory.

I think my life is a collection of blessings. Some books I have read help me see the archive of blessings with new appreciation. Yesterday I reviewed my decades-long friend Dave Norris's excellent book, *I AM,* as I made notes for a new friend who is covering a class for me this month. Dave's examination of God's loving covenant with humanity culminates in blessings. God calls His name over His people, and blessings result.

Luke 1 deserves thirty thousand words rather than the one thousand or so I will give it today. Just the way Luke links eyewitnesses and ministers in some type of parallelism where I have to see both or I have neither calls for much deeper reflection. And that phrase happens in the second of eighty verses. I feel like someone running through the Louvre on a lunch break rather than slowly giving attention to each part of a masterpiece.

The chapter includes a cacophony of sights, sounds, smells, and emotions. The evening incense closes a day of sacrifices. Devout Jews pray for God's favor as they await the priest's return to the evening shadows of the Temple's courtyard after what might have been his only opportunity to offer incense in his whole life. That was a lifetime experience made special beyond anticipation by a heavenly messenger just as the priest prostrated himself before the altar. The experience blew away anything he could have imagined.

An elder lady experiences the emotions of shame and fear being vanquished by honor and hope. When the child kicked at the voice of her cousin's greeting, decades of shame drained away. She was not cursed. She was not an evil sinner punished by God. Instead her blessing came in the autumn of life—her son would "turn the hearts of the fathers to the children, and the disobedient to the wisdom of the just; to make ready for the Lord a people prepared" (Luke 1:17). God's blessings came at the right time for her . . . and for the world.

Blessings mark you if you let them. They originate from a distant throne room, but the very Spirit of God brings them near.

This chapter echoes blessings from the past. Elizabeth was a new Sarah. John's spirit and power reflected that of Elijah and Samson. Angel visits connected God's blessings that day to many times in the past when God made His intervention visible. All the comments about turning remove the distance from Jeramiah's tear-stained writings to a season when many would see the coming King and turn toward Him. Songs of an old priest and a young girl bring to mind songs of Moses, Miriam, and Deborah. I am thankful for those who have the gift of fracturing the blessings into visible spectrums of song similar to the revealing power of a prism that surrenders to the light.

Parts of Luke 1 make us pause between the heartbeats of those immobilized by fear at a God encounter, but then the chapter ends with thirty years of John's life collapsed into one sentence. Fast or slow, every word conveys blessings.

Seeing such an avalanche of blessings drops me to my knees in thanksgiving.

---

*Dear Lord,*
*Thank you for the many waves of blessings You have poured out on my life. Each day Your blessings mold and*

*shape me into the man I want to be, but I cannot get there on my own. Like Elizabeth, I have had moments of suffering and shame along the way, but today those pains only serve to flavor Your blessings. What I or others meant for harm, You have turned into good in accordance with Your covenant goodness toward us, Your people.*

*I repent of moments when I rejected Your blessings like a pouting, recalcitrant child. Did You smile when I did that? Did You know today would come when Your blessings would overwhelm me? Did You see the tears of joy? Thank You for the years of patient mercy that continue to keep me in Your presence—even when I thought following You was more like the Mojave Desert than the garden of beauty You place around me.*

*This morning is another life experience. It came upon me so unexpectedly. I am overwhelmed by Your goodness. I want to share what I have seen—to serve out of blessings encountered. Oh Lord, Thy Kingdom come! Thy will be done! You turned so many things around in Luke 1. Those blessings still flow today.*

*In Jesus' name,*
*Amen*

---

Thank you for walking through Luke 1 with me. I trust the Master's blessings exploded all around you as you encountered the chapter with me. Even if this is a dark season for you, the jewels of God's blessings can still refract and bring twinkles of hope for tomorrow. I look forward to the rest of our walks through Luke's gospel. I wonder what delights we will discover along the way.

God bless,
Jim

# 2 | A *WALK* THROUGH LUKE 2

Back in the 1980s I did part of my student teaching in a third-grade classroom. I got to introduce children to the wonderful world of fractions. In some ways my degree, teaching credentials, and career rested on my ability to help the children learn to use fractions. For the children, and more than a few of their parents, I opened the door to a mystical mathematical world that seemed to defy logic.

I think math books should be sold at the checkout counter right next to *People* magazine. Certainly the Pythagorean theorem is more fascinating than the latest Hollywood scandal. Impulse buyers should not be able to resist mathematical beauty.

Before my students could venture into the world of algebra, geometry, and statistics, they needed to grasp and celebrate a world between whole numbers. And I got to take them there! Of course, they had experienced "less than whole" when their first bottle approached that sad sucking sound. They had reduced their parents' sleeping time to a fragment of what it had been before their blessed arrival. Cough syrup and other medicines came through little tubes with hash marks indicating parts of the whole. Fractions should be no problem for little people of normal intelligence and a vast body of experience.

Yet many of them suffered.

I lovingly explained the concepts many times. I used paper puzzles. I even pulled out the ultimate weapon—chocolate candy bars—to explain the bigger the number on the bottom (everybody say *denominator*), the smaller the fraction. Most of them got it. I passed student teaching, graduated, and got a job.

Walking through Luke 2 shows how we all experience the disorienting world of new understanding even though our truth-saturated daily lives have lain the foundations for what is to come. I marvel at God's patience as we wrestle with His commitment to reclaim all things from the brokenness of sin. Deliberately walking through the chapter makes His love palpable for me. The story unfolds right before my eyes.

God displayed His grace everywhere, yet most did not grasp it. Some people call the years between Malachi and the birth of Christ the four hundred years of silence. God has never been silent. Every sunrise and every raindrop conveyed God's love. Not only did creation declare God's ongoing conversation with humanity, the Spirit still spoke to devout men and women. Simeon and Anna heard God. Anna prophesied under the direction of the Spirit. They patiently anticipated the fulfillment of what they had heard.

With the birth of Jesus, God spoke in a new way. He chose to use questionable taxation practices to fulfill Old Testament prophecies. He sent angels to invite shepherd boys to see grace incarnate. The shepherds' revelation brought wonder to those who stood by the manger. Something about the boys' encounter caused Mary to ponder what she thought she already knew. Presenting the child at the Temple bought new understanding. Simeon blessed the parents and warned Mary of heart piercings to come.

Parenting the Christ must have brought many moments of wonder. Jesus' four-day conversation with Temple teachers brought anxiety, distress, astonishment, and deepening awareness of how little they understood their Son. Mary wisely treasured all new information in her heart even though she would not understand its meaning until decades later. This One who submitted to them continued to grow in wisdom and favor with God and humanity.

The early church could not grasp the full meaning of angelic words regarding great joy for all people and peace on earth. Simeon's prophetic words of salvation for all people groups and revelation for the Gentiles sounded as strange to the church as the new world of fractions did to my eight-year-old students.

As I walk through the chapter, I hear young angels with glittered wings grinning from ear to ear as they race through their lines beside a homemade manger placed where the pastor normally stands. How can six-year-old children in a Christmas drama understand these words? As shepherds poke each other with staffs and prance because they need to go to the bathroom, these eternal words echo through the congregation—a congregation that has heard the words often before. Parents and grandparents smile and take pictures. They fail to marvel and treasure words that have not fully come to pass. I must value these words afresh as I approach the later seasons of my life.

The wonderful truths still await their fulfillment. I have experienced Kingdom power most of my life just as children swim in a world of fractions. Though I breathe Kingdom air, I still grapple with new truths and behaviors just beyond my mental, spiritual, and emotional reach. These partially realized truths call me to pray.

---

*Dear Lord,*

*Thank You for never being silent. Sometimes Your voice booms with tidal wave strength, while at other times only patient and spiritually focused people will hear Your small voice. I worship You for the things I have heard. I repent of times I set my ear to the wrong frequency.*

*Your birth still contains truths just beyond my reach. Sometimes I feel like the shepherds; I marvel at the divine invitation to leave mundane things behind and gaze into a beautiful eternity when all creation is restored. At other times I feel like elder Simeon who sensed the Spirit's tug for decades. I believe, but I also wonder what it will be like to hold the promises in my hand.*

*Today I also feel like Mary. I have heard new things these past few months. These new things build on the foundation of truths I heard four and five decades ago. The new things bring fresh hope mingled with perplexity. I hide them in my heart.*

*Thank You for Your patience. Like a gifted math teacher, You have introduced and reinforced the wonder of Your kingdom coming and Your will being done in all the earth. My eyes sparkle with a new dawning of awareness. New faith, new trust, and a new sense of Your gifts in my life call me forward.*

*I celebrate these Kingdom impulses today, and I anticipate even more astonishment in the days to come. The pain in my heart truly does not compare to the possibilities I sense in the Spirit. Those possibilities enable me to pray, "Thy kingdom come, Thy will be done."*

*In Jesus' name,*
*Amen*

Thank you for walking through Luke 2 with me. I wish you could share some of your new experiences with the Christ child with me over a cup of coffee. As we read through the chapter, we see the footprints of all the men and women of faith who went before. Should the Lord tarry, we will also pass this way again in the future. Each immersion in the Word brings new life.

God bless,

Jim

# 3 | A *WALK* THROUGH LUKE 3

From my earliest childhood I remember expecting good things to come. What child does not look forward to birthdays and Christmas? Visits to a kind neighbor or a favorite aunt's house can ignite small anticipations of good things to come. Our daughter has to be careful about telling our grand-daughter of a pending visit with Nana—the anticipation can become too much! Our daughter's strategy is to mark the date on a calendar and ceremoniously cross off each passing day as *the* day gets closer.

I do not know if we ever outgrow anticipations and expectations. Sherri and I visited several antique stores on our anniversary getaway last week. Each case and pile of dis-carded "treasures" got careful attention. My anticipation was rewarded with a marine green Sheaffer Balance OS fountain pen from the mid-1930s in fairly decent shape and a black Sheaffer PFM 1 from the early 1960s that had very little, if any, use. I was almost embarrassed by the 50 percent discount on the PFM; it was already a good deal. After a few hours of repair, the pens will be ready to dance magically across blank pages waiting to capture the birthing of new ideas. I can hardly wait.

Sometimes life's storms and heartaches drain the human spirit of expectations like a week-old birthday balloon that has lost the energy to bounce on the ceiling. Unrealized expectations cause more divorces than arguments over money. Seeing the eyes of despair makes me want to weep with the forlorn person. In those moments I have no words of comfort; all I can do is be present in the hopelessness and trust that the Spirit will bring life once again. I also know what it is like to be held by others in the dark nights that seemed to stretch for eternity.

Perhaps C. S. Lewis captured the wonder of expectation better than any other writer in the twentieth century. His own suffering resulted from God not answering his prayer to save his beloved mother from cancer's life-draining power. At the age of ten or eleven, he gave up on God and escaped into intellectual pursuits. After witnessing the horrors of WWI—the loss of a dear friend and suffering injury himself—Lewis eventually found atheism unequal to the task of explaining why the human spirit continued to quest for joy and justice.

Lewis needed to know why people could imagine, even long for, things like beauty and peace when so little could be found. His search led him to conclude the human anticipation for the good could only come from a good God.

As I walk through Luke 3, I am shocked with the fragrance of hope emanating from a people who lived in deplorable conditions. What should have been eye-watering swamp gases of despair gave way to the divine gift of expectation for something good. God's word came to John. He preached good news to the crowds who stood on the shoulders of many generations of expectant people.

John's word of leveling and straightening the path so that all flesh could see the glory of God called them to the baptismal pool. The strangely dressed prophet offered a third alternative to the human responses of fight or flight. Rather than fleeing the wrath to come, they could bear fruit. Their best expectation—judgment avoidance—got a godly upgrade to produce good fruit. All they had to do to gain the upgrade was repent of their old perspective and behave in line with the coming glory.

When I think of good news, I automatically go to the life, death, burial, and resurrection of Jesus. Luke explained that John's words, though just a shadowy anticipation of the coming Messiah, broadcasted good news as well. His words of accountable repentance, coming judgment, and fruitful living brought good news. Perhaps his prophetic words to the Herodians brought good news to the crowd as well—they could expect that judgment would rain down on evil power brokers.

John's words about Jesus fell far short of what would come, but that is the nature of divine expectations. Humanity has a history of missed expectations; John was no exception. John saw the Holy Ghost and judgment fires collapsed into one moment; his expectations missed Jesus' third way of calling a church to continue His mission to the ends of the earth. When repentance leads us to third-way alternatives in light of the good news, our expectations will fall short of God's vision for restored humanity. We need anticipation upgrades right up to our last breath.

My expectations in light of John's good news call me to pray.

---

*Dear Lord,*

*Today I confess that all of my hopes for good things come from You. I know my hopes need adjustment to see third-way opportunities, but the fact that I expect peace, joy, and justice in this world testifies to Your redemptive care for all creation. Like John, I too have a limited perspective of what You plan to do in these last days.*

*I repent of limited expectations of deliverance and judgment against wickedness. Like the crowds, you call me to share my resources with others. Like the tax collectors, you call me to behave justly in all business practices. Like the soldiers, you call me to never misuse power and to be content with my wages.*

*The fruit I bear does not seem to be market-worthy. I can only see deformities caused by worms and early frosts, but You call me to look again. Turning away from the Kingdom impact of the fruit You produce in me rejects Your choice to use Your church to witness the inbreaking Kingdom. I repent again. I accept an expectation refresh. I feel the breath of Your Spirit as You bring renewed life to my vision.*

*Thank you for the cornea implants. Cataracts of time have clouded my expectations, but through Your Word and Spirit, I see new glimpses of light. By simply bearing the fruit You put within me, I can be a part of Your kingdom coming and Your will being done.*

*In Jesus' name,*
*Amen*

---

Thank you for walking through Luke 3 with me. Getting close to John the Baptist must have brought a shock to the nose as well as the ears, but hearing the greatest prophet made the encounter well worth it. Trust the new pinpricks of light that come from Luke 3. God challenges us to see new Kingdom possibilities each day.

God bless,

Jim

# 4 | A *WALK* THROUGH LUKE 4

Identity theft is big business for crooks, companies aimed at protecting an individual's identity, and government agencies. At one time a person could just claim to be another person and might have been able to get by with the charade. Signet rings, birth certificates, and fingerprints now give way to DNA testing, a wide range of biometrics, and digital certificates of authenticity. Some of these security measures happen behind the scenes every day, while others, like pesky password updates, bedevil us on a daily basis. I'm convinced the security measures in my life cause me more frustration than it does for a hacker who simply breaches security at my local grocery store to sell the data on the dark web.

From what I hear, recovering your identity from a modern digital highwayman can take many painstaking months to accomplish. I generally try not to think about it.

Perhaps my passport represents the most recognized and authoritative form of identity proof I have. Each decade's passport has even more security measures than the last one. My current identity booklet has so many security measures to prevent forgery that inspectors have trouble keeping track of all the details. A US passport uses sixty different materials to create the thirty-plus security measures in paper, plastic, thread, and ink. I can see the hologram, but

I do not even notice all of the ink characteristics. Even the government's font has pesky details that make counterfeiting virtually impossible. My passport carries a computer security chip; I am grateful they put it in my booklet rather than under my skin.

When I read Luke 4, I see many checks to discern Jesus' identity. From the forty days of fasting with three crucial tests to words and deeds of authority at the end of the chapter, the Spirit led the identity authentication process. With each identity check came even more authority.

Luke 4 contains Jesus' announcement of the Kingdom without the clear declaration of His own royal identity. The text conveys the strange truth that only God and demonic spirits knew the dimensions of Jesus' identity.

Even Jesus got tested.

*If* Jesus was the true authority, *then* He could end His hunger with a word that changed stones to bread. He refused the suggestion. His personal identity did not contain self-preservation and ease-of-life characteristics. He would make wonder bread for those in need. He would not feed Himself. Later in Luke's gospel, Jesus confessed that He had the power to make stones become worshipers. I am thankful He never activated that potential.

Reading the chapter causes me to wonder if the more painful test came from Jesus' experiences in His childhood synagogue. The Spirit affirmed the time had come, but the crowd asked what Jesus thought He was up to. They had waited for hundreds of years to have liberty declared at the margins of society. Now that it was time, they questioned rather than believed.

Jesus in turn challenged their faithlessness and compared them to previous generations when prophets had to look beyond Israel to bless and to heal. They rejected His words, reverted to mob mentality, and pushed him to the edge of a cliff. How quickly they moved from synagogue worship to attempted murder!

Demon-possessed and sick folks all rejoiced that Jesus' true identity was the Messiah. Just because one group of synagogue worshipers rejected His declared identity didn't mean all would. He went to preach the Kingdom to others.

As I think about my own responses to Jesus' identity, I choose a season of prayer rather than pushing Him away.

*Dear Jesus,*

*Forgive me for the many times I have questioned Your identity. Like Your childhood neighbors, I've not always responded with faith to Your message of deliverance for all who suffer. I've heard Your identity declared, yet I still see the blind, brokenhearted, rejected, bruised, and captive. Perhaps I've heard Your truths so much that I feel comfortable being the arbiter of truth.*

*Forgive me!*

*Open my ears and heart to hear again. I want to declare Your identity to those in hopelessness. I believe; help my unbelief as I pray and truly mean, "Thy kingdom come, Thy will be done, in earth as it is in heaven." I ask for the Holy Spirit to lead and empower our witness today as the Spirit did for You. Confirm our identity as Your disciples as we reject our self-identity as arbiters of truth.*

*In Jesus' name,*

*Amen*

Thank you for walking through Luke 4 with me. I hope you took the risk to hear Jesus declare His identity again. By hearing Jesus speak His identity into our situations today, we open our lives to new dimensions of His kingdom.

God bless,

Jim

# 5 | A *WALK* THROUGH LUKE 5

I have a confession to make . . . I find it challenging to follow others in traffic. Vehicles that linger in the fast lane create an unwanted emotional response. Drivers who want to go only half a mile per hour faster than the car they are passing create a parade-like following when they take several miles to return to the right-hand lane. I am an impatient, goal-oriented driver who needs to eat up miles like a factory worker doing piecework. If folks would just pay attention, accelerate more quickly, stay off their cell phones, and negotiate lane changes more efficiently, then I could get to my destination a couple of minutes earlier.

More than once I have had to just get off the road altogether to avoid my frustrating response to traffic. Why can't everyone see the highway through my perspective?

Perhaps I should remember that I am not really following anyone on the highway. I may be behind them, but I am not following them. We started from different locations, and our destinations differ. I may be traveling to visit children and grandchildren while the fellow traveler in the lane next to me may be going for a job interview a few states over. Maybe a few people still drive just to have someplace to go. We share the road. We do not share life. And I hope we do not have the opportunity to exchange phone numbers over crumpled fenders. Our paths may never cross again.

The invitation to follow Jesus represents a far different proposition!

Reading through Luke 5, I can almost smell a bouquet of the mingling odors of the sea, pitch, sweat, fish, and beasts of burden. The crowd pressed so close to Jesus that He sought access to a platform a little distant from the masses. Peter's boat became a vehicle of change far different from anything the fisherman had experienced in the past. The polite response to the young Rabbi's requisitioning of the boat changed to a less-than-enthusiastic casting of the freshly washed nets. He was in no way prepared for the burning muscles and blistered hands that resulted from a record-setting catch of fish. He could not manage the load. Even the assistance from the Zebedee boys barely spared Peter of the ignominy of sinking within the sight of the crowded shore. Confession of sin came following the miraculous catch of fish rather than the sermon.

The fishing partners could not hide their anxiety from the charismatic Teacher. Life changed for them that day. Jesus commanded their fear to leave before He prophesied their future occupation of catching men. The encounter was enough. They forsook all and followed Jesus.

The fishermen, along with the taxman later in the chapter, began the long journey to be followers of Jesus. The itinerary would bring more confessions, more startling moments, more fear, more revelations, and more invitations to participate in Jesus' mission. While they would encounter many new things over the coming years, one thing would remain a constant: they would always be followers of Jesus.

Perhaps Luke 5:26 sums up everyone's experience: "And they were all amazed, and they glorified God, and were filled with fear, saying, We have seen strange things to day."

When a leper asked for cleansing, he received far more—he received a touch from Jesus that both cleansed and healed him. Instead of getting an offer to follow Jesus, the ex-leper got a commission to witness to the priests when he went to obey the Law's cleansing ritual.

When the Pharisees and legal doctors came to evaluate the Rabbi's teaching, they too found the "power of the Lord was present to heal them" (Luke 5:17). Sadly they could not follow the moment. Instead they witnessed the rude intrusion of faith-filled men who forced everyone to make room for the paralytic. Just as the leper received cleansing prior to healing, the immobile man received redemption prior to feeling energy in his limbs.

The Pharisees evaluated everything by their own experiences rather than grasping the new Kingdom opportunities. Why surrender to the taste of Jesus' new wine when they were satisfied with making everyone see the world through their eyes?

Oh my! I see my own need to control the journey instead of following Jesus. Do I ever need to pray!

---

*Dear Jesus,*

*You are present today as I read Luke's account of the new opportunities You introduced that day. I hear the call to replace fear with the awe of Your presence to cleanse and remove sin's stains from my life and everyone I encounter. As someone who has been on Your mission for decades, I can so easily think I have found a comfortable, controllable way to travel.*

*Forgive me of my presumption! Help me to know when to listen and when to fish. Help me to know when to pray and when to feast with publicans and sinners. I really need help with this last one; I find so much joy and comfort in my church family that I really do not know how to party with sinners. Teach me the way of Levi.*

*I feel You calling me to remain open to new Kingdom possibilities that arise when I follow You. While You have already brought me a long way, I know that my fifty-five years as a disciple must not seal me off from new-wine opportunities in front of me.*

*Cleanse us and forgive us as we respond by faith. Help us to receive healing as an opportunity to show old-garment people Your power for today. As You call us from boats and tables, we will learn how to truly pray, "Thy kingdom come, Thy will be done."*

*In Jesus' name,*

*Amen*

---

Thank you for walking with me through Luke 5. I trust Luke's account comforts you as you recognize the presence of Jesus in your life today. May Luke's words also open your eyes and heart to new Kingdom possibilities. Who knows, maybe we can all be called to leave some things behind as we move to new places of witness before priests and sinners alike.

God bless,

Jim

# 6 | A *WALK* THROUGH LUKE 6

I do not know how colleges and universities choose their school mascots. I think mascots somehow rally campus members around their core values and teams while driving fear into their enemies on gridirons, hardwood floors, and ball diamonds. Somehow three of the four schools I attended are represented by birds: Jamestown Community College has the Jayhawks, Eastern Baptist Theological Seminary (now Palmer Theological Seminary at Eastern University) has the Eagles, and the University of Delaware has the Blue Hens.

The University of Delaware chose the crossbred bird as its mascot in 1911. The legislature chose the lowly blue chicken as the state bird in 1939. The inspiration came from a company of US Revolutionary War soldiers from Delaware. Evidently they fought as ferociously as their captain's entrants into cockfights. While that sport is fortunately now illegal in the US, students and alumni cheer on their mascot that is affectionately named YoUDee. Since 2010 YoUDee has won six first place and six second place finishes in national championship competitions held for mascots by the Universal Cheerleaders Association. I guess I should be a proud chicken . . . excuse me, a Fighting Blue Hen.

Walking through Luke 6 highlights two radically different teams, two ways of living. Jesus' claim to forgive sins in chapter 5 sets up the next battle with the scribes and the Pharisees. The opposition sees the Sabbath as a legal context to limit behavior and set apart those who have the luxury of living out their generations of tradition-building. Jesus claimed a new title, Lord of the Sabbath, that swept away their claim to authority over the day. Jesus let His disciples eat. Jesus healed a withered arm. His opponents had an emotional fit and channeled their energy toward destroying Jesus.

The lines were firmly drawn. Jesus was on the side of life. The other team plotted death.

Luke's special use of prayer set the stage for Jesus' selection of the twelve. He named a dozen young men apostles. While all the Lord's disciples would go on the mission, these young followers would lead the way with special authority to speak on their King's behalf. The universe must have cheered the King/Coach's decision as Jesus descended from the prayer mountain with the Twelve. The multitude heard. Diseases were healed. Unclean spirits "were vexed" and had to look for new homes. The crowd touched Jesus.

Then Jesus' words shocked all who would listen both then and now. The paradox of living in blessings by being poor, hungry, weeping, hated, and shamed for the Son of Man called for a joyful dance. The rewards were out of this world. Opposite Kingdom blessings for the chosen were woes that still turn goals for life upside down: woe be upon the rich, full, laughing, and those of good reputation.

And I thought following a blue and yellow chicken was a nonstarter!

Following Jesus formed disciples so they could be known as "children of the Highest." Surely no higher team name could be offered. Surely no greater demands could be placed on a strangely poor, weak, weeping, and blessed people. They would learn to love and bless their enemies. Most coaches point out the weaknesses of the opponents in a way that exploits and destroys. But this Coach called for returning love for hate, good for abuse, and giving with no expectation for return. Just as the Highest let rain fall on good and evil people alike, Team Jesus would love everyone they encountered.

And they would reject pride while they did it! Following Jesus lays down all moral authority to judge others because His chosen people know they still have weaknesses and limits. They will love rather than claim superior positions.

When they call Jesus "Lord," they back up their words by a lifestyle of fruitfulness. Such living provides a foundation that cannot be shaken by any storm.

Reading Jesus' actions, words, and blessings leaves me with only one response—I need to pray again.

---

*Lord Jesus,*

*Thank you for the invitation to follow You. I am overwhelmed with both the honor to be on Your team and aghast at Your playbook. Every place You promised blessings, I resist the urge to be the opposite. Every place You condemn the self-righteous, I see tendencies in me. I thought I would have all of this mastered by now since I have had over a half century as Your blessed son.*

*As I read about Your care for the broken and suffering people who flocked to You, I am astounded by the beams in my eye. You actually invited the unclean and evil-spirit-possessed people to touch You. Their eyes and noses undoubtedly ran with both pain and disease. You made the Sabbath for their healing. Virtue flowed from You with each deformed hand that touched You.*

*Now I realize that hand is attached to my arm. How are You not revolted by my faltering efforts to live out the kind of love You prescribe for Your team? Are You sure You still have a position for me so close to You?*

*I covet the kind of heart that results in acts and words of love, grace, and healing. As I pray, I see Your hand inviting me again. That invitation is the solid rock on which I want to build the remaining days of my life.*

*By Your Spirit I can love and serve others. By Your Spirit I can pray, "Thy kingdom come, Thy will be done, in earth as it is in heaven."*

*In Jesus' name,*

*Amen*

---

Thank you for walking through Luke 6 with me. I trust you also saw Coach Jesus, our Lord and Savior, reaching out an inviting hand as I did. I am sure the chapter has identified some Kingdom paradoxes that challenge you to build more firmly on the solid foundation, just as it does me. Maybe we can share a cup of coffee someday, here or by the crystal river, and talk about the wonder of being invited to live out the Kingdom in a fallen world.

God bless,

Jim

# 7 | A *WALK* THROUGH LUKE 7

On January 12, 1987, a courageous man arrived at the Beirut International Airport to negotiate the release of more hostages. A total of ninety-six people were held hostage in Lebanon between 1982 and 1992; ten of them would die before getting released. Even though Terry Waite knew he was at risk for becoming the next hostage, he could not live with an even greater risk—the risk of doing nothing when someone was in need.

Mr. Waite served as a special envoy for the Archbishop of Canterbury when he went on dangerous missions to places where others said it was hopeless. He believed he could learn to listen to anyone if he tried hard enough. Eight days into the Beirut trip, hostage takers broke their promise of safe conduct. The envoy became a hostage. He spent most of the next 1,763 days in solitary confinement. Much of that time he was chained in a dark, small cell for twenty-three hours and fifty minutes per day. Without books, papers, and news from home, Mr. Waite composed books in his mind as he made the most of each day until he was released on November 18, 1991.

Twenty years later the freed man flew back to Beirut to meet with his former captives. The mission was to find a way to move out of the past, forgive his captors, and join with them in caring for people suffering in Middle Eastern refugee camps. His lifetime of writing, humanitarian efforts, and simple conversations flow out of his lifelong passion to go into places of the greatest need.

Reading through Luke's stories recorded in chapter 7 reveals so many envoy efforts that I refuse to think it is an accident. A Roman army officer who loved the Jewish people enough to build them a synagogue felt Jewish elders would be able to convince Jesus to provide care for a dear servant who was ready to die. As Jesus drew closer to the soldier's house, friends went on his behalf. They carried words of faith that Jesus had not heard in all of Israel. The emissaries went back home to find their friend's servant completely whole again.

Mission accomplished.

The funeral crowd in Nain transformed from a mourning entourage to a worship service when they encountered a visitor on mission from God. Luke did not report the people rejoicing over the resurrected young man; he reported the crowd's acknowledgement that God's prophet-envoy had risen among them.

Mission accomplished.

John the Baptist sent representatives to Jesus because he was not able to go himself. He commissioned the two disciples to conduct a fact-finding mission: was Jesus the Promised One or should they keep looking? Jesus gave them something to take home to the prophet: the blind, lame, leprous, deaf, dead, and poor all experienced transformation.

No need to look further.

Mission accomplished.

Jesus took the opportunity to celebrate the prophet who was about to die as a Kingdom hostage. John the Baptist would not die as a failure when his death came at the end of a drunken royal orgy. John was the greatest prophet to date. But all in the kingdom of God would be greater than he. John had been a messenger going in front of the One to come. The common people and publicans rejoiced in their memory of baptism for repentance.

Mission accomplished.

The Pharisees and lawyers rejected John, repentance, baptism, and the counsel of God. They responded with a no.

Mission accomplished. They had heard the word.

Luke further unpacks the Pharisees' rejection of Envoy John's words by letting us observe a dinner party at Simon's house. Simon offered no water for Jesus' feet, no kiss of welcome, and no ointment of honor at the end of the day. In contrast, the sinner woman washed the feet with her tears and ceaselessly kissed those same feet as she lavishly lathered Him with ointment from the alabaster box. Jesus forgave her much; she loved much. Simon maintained his superior state and loved little. The lady with hair disheveled by its use in washing, eyes rimmed in red from tears, and wealth depleted by worship went home in peace. Her peace would radiate out as a gift of Jesus' loving forgiveness.

Mission accomplished.

Evangelist Luke accomplished his mission again. Consuming chapter 7 leaves me with no option but to pray.

---

*Lord Jesus,*

*I receive Luke's words as communication from above. Thank You for the biblical writers who faithfully fulfilled their missionary work in the world. Today I am humbled again by their words. How do I deserve receiving Heaven's emissaries? Even more so, how can I even grasp the work of the Holy Spirit as a witnessing presence equal to that which the disrupted funeral procession encountered?*

*Forgive and change the things in my life that limit my response to Your Word and Spirit. I quest for deeper awareness of how much I have been forgiven, how much I am graciously loved. As I receive Your grace, I humbly receive Your promise that the least in the Kingdom like me can have a greater impact than Envoy John the Baptist.*

*I go from Word and prayer in the same peace that emanated from the woman with the alabaster box. You send me, but You do not send me alone. The Comforter goes with me and guides me. My brothers and sisters go with me as well. I look forward to the day when the harvest is gathered and we hear, "Well done, good and faithful servant."*

*I believe mission accomplishment is in progress as we pray "Thy kingdom come, Thy will be done."*

*In Jesus' name,*
*Amen*

---

Thank you for walking with me through Luke 7. I trust you can identify many ways the Lord has sent messengers into your life. I pray you have joined with me in repentance and acceptance of your envoy mission. Walk in peace. Your message will be noticed.

God bless,

Jim

# 8 | A *WALK* THROUGH LUKE 8

The Lord has blessed Sherri and me with the privilege of traveling to many beautiful places over the past forty years. Several years ago we had the opportunity to spend a couple of months in the great Northwest. As with most trips, we found the journey to be filled with delightful surprises along the way to our destination. Once we turned north from Kansas City we were in new territory. Saint Joseph, Missouri, had reminders of days gone by when westward traveling migrants would take months to reach their destination rather than the five days we allotted ourselves. We saw where the Pony Express riders spurred their horses on the first leg of their journey. Of course I had to stop at the Stetson factory outlet store in search of the perfect fedora . . . or five.

From Saint Joseph the Missouri River was on our left as we continued northward. A little while later, Sherri noted a sign that said Nebraska was just across the river. I muttered something insignificant like, "Yes, indeed," and drove forward to consume the number of concrete miles we had set for the day.

The temperature in the truck seemed to get a little colder with each mile. Conversation lagged. My smiling glances at the beauty of my life did not get the wink that still makes my heart flutter.

My many years of studying human behavior helped me reach a helpful conclusion: I had made a mistake somewhere during the day. Unfortunately I must have missed the day that covered husband etiquette while on a road trip. Some time later I finally got an answer to why my driver's seat had become a doghouse while traveling 70 mph.

I failed to hear correctly when Sherri said, "There is Nebraska." I heard a detail of geography. She intended for me to hear that she would like to spend ten minutes crossing the bridge to Nebraska so that she could cross it off along with South Dakota, Montana, Washington, and other states on the way home. Each checked-off state represented progress toward hitting all fifty.

I couldn't hear what she was saying. Even though I made up for the faux pas the next summer with a drive to the missed state, a "Nebraska" will always mean I am not listening properly.

As I walk through Luke 8, I am struck by the many ways folks failed to truly hear Jesus. The twelve disciples and the women who had experienced deliverance from evil spirits and infirmities traveled with Him as He went "preaching and shewing the glad tidings of the kingdom of God" (Luke 8:1). That which had occupied everyone's hopes for so long had finally arrived!

Jesus' parable about the sower, seed, and soil ended with the warning, "Take heed therefore how ye hear" (Luke 8:18). As beautiful as the message of Kingdom liberation might be, some would not respond to the sown Word. While the Word will never return void, in some cases the soil will not hold the Word with patience until it produces fruit. How could broken human beings not hear the message of glad tidings?

- Wayside places are more conducive to seed thieves than fruit production.

- Stony places allow for momentary joy, but not root development to sustain life when temptations come along.

- Hearers that make space for both the Word and the cares, riches, and pleasures of this life experience strangulation before fruit is produced.

- Praise God, good ground keeps the Word and brings forth fruit because honest and good hearts have patience to nourish the fruit for the whole season.

Hearing and doing the Word of God provide the DNA needed to form the new Kingdom family that follows Jesus. With heavy heart I think of natural families that experience rupture when cares-of-life soil and fruitful soil exist in the same household. The soil differences create family estrangement in so many cases.

Luke's artful telling of the story shows the reader that storms and demons have no choice but to hear when Jesus speaks. Waves defied the physics of motion when Jesus spoke. Demons abandoned the outcast among the tombs in an instant at the command of Jesus.

Luke also vividly shows that people have a choice in the matter. One would think the ex-demoniac's town would welcome the Miracle Worker and experience wider circles of Kingdom talk. But they were more concerned about their pigs than their outcasts. Jesus left the man behind to see if any good ground could be found for the Kingdom message while He answered their prayer and cast off from their shore.

Fortunately Jairus, a ruler in the synagogue, and the isolated hemorrhagic woman heard Jesus was coming and acted in faith. The woman persisted in hearing Kingdom possibilities and pressed through until virtue restored her body to a condition she had forgotten in more than a decade of weakness. Jairus's good and honest heart called for further intervention from Jesus. His words had changed weepers into mocking scorners, so He had to help the man close the door on other voices. Jairus never regretted tuning out the laughter in favor of two simple words, "Maid, arise."

As I read through Luke, I face a choice. I can critically analyze the threaded stories to maintain some semblance of objectivity that makes me think I am in control, or I can listen. I mean really listen. I do not want today to be another "Nebraska."

Such listening calls me to prayer.

---

*Lord Jesus,*

*You know my heart like no one else does . . . even better than I do. Your voice always speaks with truth and power, but sometimes my hardness of self-preservation, self-esteem, and self-efficacy seal me off from experiencing Kingdom life found in Your Word. I have done it before; I have treasured those three pigs of self over the everlasting life that comes from surrendering my will and following You.*

*Have mercy, O Lord! Your garment is within reach. I feel life being restored with hope and joy as You change my name from "somebody" in the crowd to "Son." Thank You!*

*I pray, "Thy kingdom come, Thy will be done, in earth as it is in heaven." As I pray, I feel strength in my hands and in my voice—strength to serve others in Your name and to testify of Your goodness. If You can heal me, then You can heal anyone!*

*In Jesus' name,*
*Amen*

---

Thank you for walking with me through Luke 8. I trust you have heard His voice speak good tidings of the kingdom of God for your life right where you are. I pray you privilege that voice above all static that seeks to pull you from God's kingdom purposes in your life.

God bless,

Jim

# 9 | A *WALK* THROUGH LUKE 9

I think men have been fascinated with power tools from the beginning. Naming the elephant must have included a recognition of the power the massive pachyderms possessed. Perhaps efforts to domesticate the beasts and harness their power for use began in the Garden. At least as early as four thousand years ago, elephants served their trainers in India.

While I've never ridden an elephant or needed one to accomplish a task, I've been enamored with power tools on many occasions. Cutting grass, felling trees, waxing floors, and brushing my teeth have all called for power tools. The tool industry now provides interchangeable power packs to "enable" men's need for tools while removing most power cords. What a beautiful thing! How much more work can be accomplished now that I can set screws and pound nails without wearing out my arm as I did when my brothers and I helped Dad build houses back in the day.

As I walk through Luke 9, I am astounded by Kingdom power and how it deviates from our normal perception of power. The chapter relentlessly dismantles "normal" power domesticated by human beings to help us surrender to the power Jesus uses to restore all creation to Himself. When I observe the overwhelming magnitude of God's mission in the church, I can too easily look in the wrong direction for the resources to complete the task. Jesus sent the Twelve on a mission with full power but with no tangible resources. They had power and authority over all devils and diseases as they preached the Kingdom and healed the sick, but they had nothing for the journey. They traveled light as they walked in full Kingdom power.

When the Twelve returned from their power-packed field trip, they experienced another power moment when Jesus fed the massive crowd with five loaves and two fish. They were flat broke, but they each had a basket filled with leftover fragments.

Luke masterfully brackets power revelations by prayer meetings. The first prayer meeting preceded the revelation of Jesus' identity as "The Christ of God," and the second ended with an appearance of Moses and Elijah. No wonder Peter suggested they build a few tabernacles on the mountain to commemorate the event. Moses' earlier trip up a mountain encountered God's glory in the cloud and ended with the construction of a tabernacle. As Peter and the other two disciples stood powerless as the cloud enveloped them, they must have felt as well as heard God's voice, "This is my beloved Son: hear him" (Luke 9:35).

The first revelation ended with a declared power reversal: "the Christ of God" will suffer, be rejected by the power brokers, be assassinated, and will rise on the third day.

The second revelation ended with a power failure: disciples who could earlier cast out demons and heal all manner of sickness were helpless to care for a man and his possessed son. Refusing to accept Jesus' inverted power plan robbed them of their faith and put them in the classification of "perverse generation" (Luke 9:41). Resisting Jesus' call to pick up the cross daily and follow Him results in a twisted, crooked, perverted, distorted, and warped way of following Jesus.

Such distorted faith resulted in catastrophic results in addition to the immediate failure to free the boy:

- The disciples fought for power to be the greatest.

- They wanted to own the franchise on Jesus' power and prevent others from exercising spiritual power.

- They turned from Jesus' mission to save others when a strange spirit caused them to want to bring destruction on a village that rejected Jesus.

Refusing to accept Jesus' inversion of "normal" power systems caused them to be momentarily under the influence of an evil spirit!

Lord, have mercy! I must respond to Jesus' call to prayer.

---

*Oh Lord,*

*Your kingdom always comes with authority and power! Always! Yet I find myself seeking alternative power sources. When under the influence of perverted power, I think money, social power, buildings, technology, and a different set of people than those with whom I serve right now are needed to see the influences of sin and shame crushed in the world around me.*

*Like the disciples, I have heard You say, "Follow Me!" As a young disciple the simple call filled me with excitement and Kingdom possibilities. Now I hear the next call that You issue to everyone who has ever left a boat, tax table, or family comfort: "If any man will come after me, let him deny himself, and take up his cross daily, and follow me" (Luke 9:23).*

*In my perversion I think cross carrying is for just a moment of testing and purification. Yet You insist it is the only way for Kingdom power to be at work in Your people. Meanwhile competition, inability to care for others, defending my control of Your power, and preference of vindicating judgment over redemption creep into my operating system by some "strange spirit"—the spirit of false kingdom power.*

*Thank You for Your healing touch! I will eat again out of the miracle basket and remember that true power inverts all around me. Only then can I pray, "Thy kingdom come, Thy will be done."*

*In Jesus' name,*

*Amen*

---

Thank you for walking with me through Luke 9. Maybe your trip through the chapter was not quite as ugly as mine was, but I am certain true Kingdom power called you closer to the Christ and your daily cross. I pray you courageously turn your back on all power but that which comes from above.

God bless,

Jim

# 10 | A *WALK* THROUGH LUKE 10

Einstein was not that different from ancient thinkers and modern artists. Einstein worked the last few decades of his life to develop a unified theory or formula that could explain everything in the physical world. The ancient peoples looked for ways to break down the world around them into basic elements. Babylonians saw everything being derived from water, fire, earth, sea, and sky. For Greeks it was earth, water, air, and fire. The Chinese kept fire, earth, and water, but they added metal and wood to the list. Medieval alchemists added ether, sulfur, mercury, and salt to the basic Greek four.

Artists have a different view of the world. Painters look for color, line, shape, form, texture, point, space, and value as building blocks to represent the world. On the other hand, musicians think in categories such as melody, texture, rhythm, form, harmony, dynamics, timbre, and tonality. I am sure architects, sculptors, and creators of metaverse "worlds" have their own categories.

Physicians, economists, anthropologists, and kinesiologists all have their categories as well. Each discipline requires years of formal and informal training to master seeing the world through their respective lenses and acting appropriately as part of their guild.

As I look at the genius construction of Luke 10, I marvel at the beauty of a life fixed on following Jesus. By recounting the events of three simple encounters, Luke captures disciple-guiding principles that could occupy all followers of Jesus for their rest of their lives. Perhaps chapter ten's focus on right practices parallels Luke's Sermon on the Plain's teaching on right thinking about the Kingdom.

Act One captures Jesus' sending of the seventy to go in front of Him. This group of followers are not the core twelve apostles—no, they are normal disciples. Normal disciples who accept the challenge to pray and live in light of Kingdom service. Normal disciples who reject average thinking and live in favor of simply acting normally at the Master's command. They would both *pray* for laborers in the field and *become* those very laborers. Since normal disciples base their lives on Jesus' Word, they can go defenseless and bereft of alternative resources. Rather than wheeling suitcases for the journey, they carried words of peace and the nearness of the Kingdom. Living in this way freed them from taking victories and rejections personally. They merely represented the One to come.

What is the result of normal disciple living? Devils surrendered to His name. Serpents, scorpions, and the enemy were robbed of their poisons. And normal disciples learned to rejoice over having their name in the Book rather than appearing successful. As babies they have received Kingdom wisdom and authority. Normal disciples live more blessed than all the prophets and kings that had gone before. They announced Jesus rather than themselves.

Act Two from Luke 10 may tell the story of a self-justifying elite member of society, but Jesus turned the lawyer's attempt to demonstrate his superiority to Jesus into an opportunity to highlight another normal disciple behavior: living out the twin love commands. The man easily understood the words of the great commandments that produce eternal life, but he was unable to put his understanding into practice. All self-justifiers invalidate their discipleship. Normal disciples demonstrate their love of God and love of neighbor by actually living like a neighbor. The Samaritan's compassion for the wounded man surpassed mere understanding of the need.

The Samaritan exercised margins in his finances, time, and emotions by actively living as a loving neighbor.

Act Three reinforces the foundation for normal disciple living. Martha could keep busy with work. Jesus said she was careful and troubled about many things. Her sister chose the core identity of disciple over being defined by labors of the moment. She dared risk being a disciple of Jesus—a role unavailable to women in her day.

The inbreaking of the Kingdom calls all disciples to experience the joy of having their name in the Book, finding love fulfilled in serving someone in need, and prioritizing their identity in Christ above all else.

Oh, boy, does the possibility of being a normal disciple drive me to pray!

---

*Dear Lord,*

*Like Chorazin, Bethsaida, and Capernaum, I have seen mighty Kingdom exploits at so many points in my life. Rather than judging cities with Sodom-like behaviors as worthy of destruction, I repent that my life has not fully lived up to the Kingdom potentials of Luke 10. Surely if Sodom's inhabitants had seen unbelievable Kingdom transformations like I have, they would have zealously lived for Jesus rather than for their own selfish desires.*

*I pray for twenty-first-century field hands. Some of the white fields are filled with amber waves of grain. Other fields are white with lighted skyscrapers and a tangled web of highways with people scurrying in failed attempts to find meaning. I pray that we hear Your call to be normal disciples in this season. I pray we quit thinking that we do not have resources for urban rebirth of the church when what we need is Kingdom power rather than extra bank accounts, loft apartments, and gilded lifestyles.*

*Baptize me with love for You that consumes me with compassion for those You have placed within my reach. I surrender my self-satisfaction by observing the bounty You have placed in my hands to care for others in need. I really do not want to live in any way other than as a disciple focused on being like You.*

*As I live as this kind of Kingdom disciple, I can join with my brothers and sisters to pray, "Thy kingdom come, Thy will be done." Start in us!*

*In Jesus' name,*
*Amen*

---

Thank you for walking with me through Luke 10. I believe meditating on these three normal disciple scenes can transform our minds, actions, and emotions. The Holy Spirit will lead you in taking the next steps in the disciple journey.

God bless,
Jim

# 11 | A *WALK* THROUGH LUKE 11

I follow daily routines like most people do. If I do not put my wallet in my pocket at the right point in my morning routine, then I may spend the whole day without it. I like a few cups of French press coffee in the morning. Sharing cups of espresso with my brother (Dr. Dan, assistant professor of music at Urshan College) after lunch signals the middle of the day and the gift of fellowship.

As Sherri and I begin this new phase of ministry, we realize some of our routines and traditions will have to be discarded or morphed into something fit for this season of life. I mourned the passing of one of those traditions this morning. For well over a decade I have looked forward to serving Sherri breakfast in bed on Sunday morning. Pulling back the curtain and handing her breakfast (from a very limited menu, I guarantee) celebrates our love for each other. Life brings many changes, but our love deepens.

This morning I realized I am scheduled to be out of town for the next eight Sundays. I anticipate the number will extend beyond that. Sherri will get to go with me on some of the trips, but a few of the Sundays she will have a quiet house to herself. No one will pull back the curtain. No one will bring the breakfast. Love will continue, but the valued tradition will have to change to meet the life situation. While I mourn the loss of one tradition, I look forward to co-authoring another one with my special lady!

As I read through Luke 11, I see two ways to address the changes that Jesus brings to us: we can either ask Him to teach us new behaviors, or we can expend our energy trying to find fault with Him while justifying ourselves. I wish I could say my tradition is to always follow Jesus, but I try not to lie. Sometimes I continue in a practice, belief, and attitude while the Holy Spirit lovingly calls me to change. Sometimes I embrace the change. At other times I pout.

Luke 11 shows the power of embracing Jesus' presence. Prayer changes us to seek Kingdom purposes rather than our own. The asking, seeking, and knocking story comes alive only for those who receive others into their lives. Pounding on a neighbor's door for food demonstrates persistence for a friend in need. The food would not satisfy a personal midnight hunger attack—the food had to be available as part of being hospitable to a traveler.

Do I seek the Father's good gifts, especially the Holy Spirit (Luke 11:13), to feed those in need who cross my path or to make my life more enjoyable? Will I change both my prayer list and persistence to line up with Jesus?

Will I enjoy relationship with Jesus, but privilege the blessings that come from hearing and keeping the Word of God (Luke 11:27–28)? Will this light bring joy to my life by hoarding it or by treasuring the opportunity for light to shine into the darkness around me (Luke 11:29–36)? Will I congratulate myself for looking clean on the outside while paving over corruption in my own inner being? I do keep a tradition of being "clean" on the outside, but focusing on that minor part of holiness lets me ignore the more important matters of justice and actively loving God and others. Letting others think they can follow my external purity camouflages a corrupted lifestyle to such an extent that others will fall into the same trap (Luke 11:39–44).

Being near Jesus brings great comfort and challenges at the same time. Such nearness reinforces some parts of my life while urging me to change in other areas. The Spirit is beckoning me to be more like Jesus. I need to pray.

*Dear Jesus,*

*Thank you for being so near today! I celebrate the opportunity to teach a Sunday school class and to worship with the saints. As I enjoy these tradition gifts, I seek greater faithfulness to Your example. I am sorry for times when I resist, seek to protect myself, and fail to see an open door to love others and do justice. Sometimes I make myself feel more comfortable by saying I am too busy to incorporate these traditions deeper into my spirit and daily life. Sometimes racing through my week helps me hear the tires hum over the sighing of a neighbor in need. Keeping my eyes on the road ahead keeps me from acting justly today.*

*I know You call me "Son." I know You love me more now than when I started. These are the reasons I want to be more like You. I like traditions of prayer. You and I have done this for many years. Today, however, You remind me that persistent prayer should be for others rather than for myself. Your holiness exposes deeper places in my spirit that I cannot hide behind my long sleeves. I pray for deeper holiness in my life—the kind that puts traffic cones around the potholes of life rather than making them into traps for others.*

*Oh, how I wish to shine even more brightly for You! I pledge to use this season of change in my life to do so. With the Holy Spirit calling, leading, and equipping me, I know new traditions will bring You even more glory. I respond by praying, "Thy kingdom come, Thy will be done!"*

*In Jesus' name,*

*Amen*

Thank you for walking with me through Luke 11. Perhaps we can all find new traditions as we live and pray the Word. These changes will not always come easily, but we can do it together! By the way, I also look forward to a new tradition to show Sherri how special she is to me. I wonder how long it will take.

God bless,

Jim

# 12 | A *WALK* THROUGH LUKE 12

Serving as a substitute kindergarten teacher frequently brought delightful moments, as you can imagine. I miss those oversized books I used for group reading exercises, and sharing time provided many surprises! Coordinating bathroom breaks and snack times either developed the teacher's logistic skills or sent them to a hermit's hut. I asked students to take a nap in those days; years later my college students would take the initiative to nap on their own during my three-hour lectures.

Good lesson plans helped me survive in those days. The year's first snowfall, however, brought on what I call GADD, or Generalized Attention Deficit Disorder. Lesson plans lost their strategic significance. Big books and calendar time lost their luster as millions of miracles fell from the sky. Mortal teachers lost their influence as well. Janitors had extra duty cleaning the windows of little nose prints and Play Doh-infused dermal ridges. None of us could pay attention to the strategically planned educational activities.

Luke 12 reminds me of those first snowfalls. Kindergarten Teacher Jesus tried desperately to guide the trampling crowd out of their GADD. The Teacher began with "Beware" and ended the lengthy chapter with "Give diligence." In between He pointed out dangerous pitfalls set up by false teachers, sidetracking pleasures, and dark motives such as covetousness, anxieties, and leadership abuses.

As a great teacher, He sought to give them something more constructive to observe. He pointed out God's super-intending care that even counted their hairs, the Holy Spirit's ability to provide words in court cases, and the Father's good pleasure to deliver the Kingdom. Jesus also spoke of discerning the time—a time with pending judgment. Such judgment would bring punishment or rich reward depending on the servant's stewardship.

While snowflakes deserve every kindergartener's attention, and their teacher's attention as well I might add, spiritual GADD seriously hinders spiritual maturation. When I attend to hurtful attacks of others more than my value to the Father, poor emotional and behavioral outcomes will always follow. When my energy expenditure revolves around hoarding resources for fear that I will not have food or clothing, I overlook the opportunity to give alms to those in need. In short, I start acting like the world and its GADD. Amid the static that threatens to overwhelm me, I hear the call to prayer.

---

*Dear Jesus,*

*I think today could be Christmas Day if I only look where You point. Your presence patiently guides my every step, thought, and emotion. I wonder what gifts are in store for Your children today as we focus on Your purposes rather than our own? Show us the sparkling of Your presence, I pray. Forgive me of my momentary GADD. I never feared Your love would leave when the cares of life distract me, but I do know You desire far more flourishing moments in my life. Living abundantly comes only from attending to Your kingdom principles.*

*Today presents many chores for me to accomplish. I lay my head on the pillow last night in anticipatory exhaustion over what is to come. I dedicate this day to You. I pray, "Your kingdom come, Your will be done." Perhaps I'll breathe again.*

*My mother taught me a song before I ever went to school. She sang, "Watch your eyes, watch your eyes, what they see." Sometimes I feel good when that applies to media consumption, but sometimes I even fail then. Hearing Your voice this morning reminds me that You have set far better things before my eyes. These better things will shrink my fears and expand my capacity for joyful service. By Your grace I will have a better outlook today. If I do it today and tomorrow, if I walk with others in this way, then I will more clearly see Your kingdom outbreaking all around me.*

*Lord, today I lay aside designs for bigger barns. Instead help me to attend to "bags which wax not old" (Luke 12:33). Who knew a bag can hold more treasure than bigger barns? Will you guide my alms-giving in ways that provide care for another one of Your children? Maybe showing them this kind of Jesus will give them a glimpse of the love and hope they long for but have failed to find. Maybe they too can learn to hear Your voice calling them to a better way.*

*I think I can learn. I believe; help Thou my unbelief. I listen; help Thou my GADD.*

*In Jesus' name,*
*Amen*

Thank you for walking with me through Luke 12. Perhaps the passage speaks to some area of GADD in your life as well. James 5 tells us we can experience healing if we confess these faults one to another. Fervent prayer still avails much!

God bless,

Jim

# 13 | A *WALK* THROUGH LUKE 13

During my childhood, Dad followed two of Jesus' professions. Dad served others by preaching the gospel and by working as a carpenter. My brothers and I learned quickly to hold hammers, climb ladders, pour concrete, and deliver sermons. I think I have the sequence right. My first hammer hold did not go well. I used the hammer to break out those cool little glass windows in a borrowed carpenter's level. For some reason Dad remembers that accomplishment to this day.

I enjoyed most parts of construction. Who wouldn't like using power tools and seeing a wall appear by the end of the day? I found working on a project with Dad to be more enjoyable than going to an amusement park. Perhaps I found more fun in mastering a new skill than in working hard to control certain bodily reflexes when going through loops and spins. I think I am still a bit like that today.

Some parts of construction were not so fun. I found the less desirable parts at the bottom and top of the house. I really did not like the heavy mud work. All that muck and very little beauty did not appeal to me for some reason. Of course, I knew from both of Dad's professions that a good foundation makes everything else possible. So I dug and sweated. I also found out that blisters only last a little while.

The top side of the house presented another challenge. I did not mind climbing. Littles boys come in two variations— some of us gladly climb ladders and others experience oxygen deprivation when standing on tippy toes. For me the ladder was fine. The problem, however, was what you got to carry up the ladder. Shingles get carried by boys who cannot nail them down. You start with part of a bundle, and then you graduate to the full bundle. Fortunately the old days are gone; shingles now get delivered to the rooftop.

Shingles bend the back. Shingles hurt. As I read Luke 13 I feel for the bent woman. I wonder what "spirit of infirmity" had broken her posture and possibly her spirit (Luke 13:11). I wonder how many looked on her with pity. They could stare with no fear of being observed because the lady could not lift her head. She only saw the footprints left by others and perhaps a crushed flower from time to time.

Even with her bent back she had courage. Jesus found her in the synagogue on the Sabbath. In that moment the bending of eighteen years evaporated. The first face she saw showed compassion. As she rested from her labors that day, she saw the One who transforms lives. Perhaps she had trouble understanding the fuss that ensued. Why was the synagogue president so angry? Maybe if he had walked her path, he would have celebrated with her. She listened to Jesus as He argued her worth to those who valued her less than a beast of burden.

Jesus valued her.

Jesus went on to teach the wonder of the kingdom of God. The Kingdom would start as a little seed and grow into a tree to lodge birds. The Kingdom would be like Mom's homemade bread. The dough would keep rising even after she punched it down a couple of times. The yeast did that. The Kingdom would go into the world and change everything!

Yet not all would be changed. Some would not go through the straight gate; they would enjoy the bread and fish on the outside. They would even listen to Jesus' teaching, but His wisdom could not coax them to walk through to the Kingdom.

Jesus lamented.

Jesus wanted to heal more bent people. Jesus wanted to feed the soul in addition to the body. Jesus wanted all He met to know they had value regardless of what others said.

But some would not step under His wing. I hear the call to prayer to make sure I am ready to receive the healing Jesus has in store for me.

---

*Dear Jesus,*

*Thank You for Your Word today. You have lifted my gaze and healed me so many times. Yet I wonder how often I do not show up on the Sabbath where You want to do some of Your best work. Forgive me, I pray. I do go to church. I do not always rest. Instead I let the shingles of life push me down. Infirmities bend me over.*

*Help me to take more Sabbaths where You wait for me. Rather than seeing rest as escape from work, help me to see rest as an opportunity to see You and to know my life has value. I know from the reading a few days ago that I will get to carry my cross as I follow You; however, I know that cross is not worry, fear, worthlessness, loneliness, hopelessness, or aimlessness. I can carry my cross, but these other things cripple me. They cripple me to such an extent that I cannot help others—and You know I want to do that more than I want to go to an amusement park or a beach resort.*

*I hear Your voice again this morning. I pause from my work. I remember a few years ago when You healed me of my own eighteen-year infirmity. You want to do it again. I receive Your invitation to walk through the straight gate.*

*I receive the healing that only rest in Your presence can provide. I look forward to more Sabbaths with You and Your people.*

*In Jesus' name,*

*(I mean it Lord; I will need Your help to rest from my work so that You can do Yours. Let Your kingdom be on earth as it is in Heaven.)*

*Amen*

---

Thank you for walking with me through Luke 13. Maybe you could take a moment of rest today. Do not be surprised if Jesus raises you up and you see Him for the first time in a long while.

God bless,

Jim

# 14 | A *WALK* THROUGH LUKE 14

I do not think my condition comes under the protection of the Americans with Disabilities Act, but I certainly am party challenged. Somewhere along the line I did not get the social script for attending events designated as a party. More than once I have suggested I need to have one of my children give me an "urgent" phone call in case I felt a little trapped and out of place. I usually rely on Sherri to help me know how long I need to stay and when leaving is acceptable. I sometimes fear the things I talk about are either esoteric fountain pen geekdom or subjects where I fall into professor mode with a three-hour lecture in mind. I generally wind up apologizing for both at some point.

Party guests sometimes bring challenges. I am not the only one, I am sure! Jesus represented another kind of challenge. He loved people too much to either stay away from parties or to stay silent. Jesus did His best work at parties! Luke 14 records Jesus' teaching at a formal, invitation-only affair as well as the post-party roadside conversation.

I appreciate Jesus' keen assessment of human behavior at parties. I often spend a little time conducting social interaction research myself in those moments. I jokingly tell people I may be more suited for writing about parties than attending them. On this particular Sabbath, Jesus accepted an invite to the house of one of the chief Pharisees. They came to watch their guest who tended to break social conventions. Jesus did not disappoint the crowd of semi-uptight attendees. Rather than a parlor trick, Jesus healed a man with serious fluid buildup. What they could not see was Jesus' even greater work to heal the far more serious heart problem.

Good party guests always have stories to tell. Again, Jesus did not disappoint. When Jesus spoke, however, His words had power. His words convicted. His words called for humility and loving responses. While Jesus' words could bring peace and comfort, He did not use those words with the uptight crowd. This crowd wanted the best rooms and the seats of honor. This crowd only ate with respectable people. This crowd only followed social protocols derived from pride and control.

I hear Jesus today. He wants to heal us of so much! That healing, however, comes to the humble and the outcast.

I hear Jesus today. He wants us to open our lives to others. That opening, however, becomes a heavenly enterprise when it provides access for those at the margins or in need.

I hear Jesus today. He sends us to those we would not have thought of as "preferred" guests.

I hear Jesus today. He asks us again if we have considered the cost of discipleship. He wants to know if our quest to follow Him reigns supreme over everything else.

I hear Jesus today . . . His words call me to prayer.

---

*Dear Jesus,*

*You have been so good to me! I do not deserve to be a part of Your body, the church. I do not deserve to hear Your voice and feel Your Spirit along with the saints. Forgive me, I plead, for times when I wanted respect from others rather than wanting to live respectfully as Your son. Forgive me, I plead, for times when I took offense when I was overlooked or overshadowed by others. Forgive me, I pray.*

*If I can accept the small room, the children's table, then maybe I will be better suited to invite people who never even get to come to the party. Maybe I will see the outcast instead of looking beyond them in my rush to do important stuff. By Your Spirit I could even offer an invitation from the King to a wounded child of Yours who thinks his scars, bruises, and coping strategies disqualify him from polite society. You still offer those invitations today, don't You? Can I carry one?*

*I have been in a bit of a tight spot lately. I know You are near. I know You love. I know You call in a still small voice. I also know at times I push You away for fear of where discipleship may take me in this next season of my life. Today, Jesus, I feel like the unwanted wayside man. You have called, but I have resisted. Today, Jesus, I surrender again my wishes, pride, and claims for respectability.*

*I surrender all I have to just be Your disciple. I trust You even though it feels so risky. Today is a good day to reconsider the cost of it all. I started building the tower and fighting the fight in faith. I said yes to the cost many years ago. Maybe I did not know today's cost when I started, but I still believe I made the right choice back then. I think the stack of used calendars and shelves of filled journals have brought me to a place where I can trust You even more.*

*How can I say thank You for coming to the party? Seeing You today gives me the courage to pray, "Thy kingdom come, Thy will be done."*

*In Jesus' name,*
*Amen*

Thank you for walking with me through Luke 14. I hope walking with an awkward non-party guy has not been too painful. While I struggle with parties, I deeply enjoy sharing a cup of coffee with a few folks. Maybe we can share a cup someday and talk about how good God has been and how He loves us enough to call us to new places of discipleship. Maybe we will not get that chance here, but I know we will all enjoy the Last Big Party in the Father's house. I cannot wait to see who you bring from the streets with you on that day! I know the Lord will make them feel welcome . . . after all, He invited me again today.

God bless,

Jim

# 15 | A *WALK* THROUGH LUKE 15

In 1971 Carole King wrote and sang the song "So Far Away" as part of her hit album *Tapestry*. Her song spoke to a period of US history filled with lost dreams and hopes unfulfilled. The 1960s called for new possibilities of human fulfillment. We put men on the moon, but we could not stop the violence in the streets or in Southeast Asia. Ms. King's song seems to carry some personal pain in losses of relationship in a mobile society. For example, she asks repeatedly, "Doesn't anybody stay in one place anymore?"

On the same album, Ms. King promises to come running when "you just call out my name" in the song "You've Got a Friend." Perhaps the melancholy of the reality that she cannot be that friend to everyone is reflected in the lyrics of the album's title song, "Tapestry." A drifting man of fortune wanders aimlessly past her and becomes part of the fabric of her life. When the man in the patchwork coat comes away empty-handed after reaching for golden fruit on a tree, he sits down on a rock and succumbs to a curse. The singer laments, "I wept to see him suffer, though I didn't know him well." In her sorrowful, lonely eulogy to a stranger, the singer's tapestry of life unravels.

Perhaps that album from forty-five years ago speaks even more profoundly to our world today. The mobility of American culture now adds roughly 14 percent foreign-born people (4.7 percent in 1970) to continental migration patterns of those born in the US. According to the US census bureau, about one in nine people move every year, perhaps reminding us of Ms. King's question: "Doesn't anybody stay in one place anymore?"

Reading through Luke 15, we see a shift in scenes from the previous chapter. Rather than eating with privileged people, the outcasts have come to Jesus. Perhaps Jesus multiplied the bread again or everyone just shared what little food they had. Then the "good" people complained that Jesus received and ate with sinners. Meanwhile Jesus told three more stories that all included lost things: a poor shepherd's sheep, a lady's silver coin, and a father's son.

When the searchers located what they had lost, they called their friends for a celebration. It did not matter that the sheep knew it was lost but could not find the way home, that the coin had no awareness of its lostness, or that the son had to come to his senses and find his own way home—someone called for a celebration in each story.

Maybe Carole King does not travel the road alone. Maybe some folks have cried for the Shepherd so long that they cannot bleat anymore. Maybe some do not even have a hope that things can be any different. Lost simply describes a condition without any thought of a searcher. Maybe some have dishonored the Father and walked away, but they fear facing shame and potential rejection when they wonder if coming home is even possible. They fear reaching for the golden fruit of belonging, only to be rejected and cursed one more time.

I travel quite a bit these days. When people ask where I am from, I generally answer with a reference to the last city I visited. I have to put the hotel room key envelope in my pocket or I will forget which room was mine. Fortunately each place I visit becomes a new home, a new place of celebration. Each worship service and shared meal reminds me that I belong to a really big family. The Father prepares a place to welcome us home very soon. What a celebration that will be! The anticipation calls me to prayer.

---

*Dear Jesus,*

*I know some people who used to worship with us. They experienced the wonder of healing and belonging. Perhaps the path grew difficult, the safety net broke, or they thought staying in the house meant they would miss out on so many pleasures of the world. The conditions do not matter; they all deserve a Searcher. You call and welcome all home.*

*I am sorry for the times when I felt the loss as something about me rather than about the one lost. In those times I searched for a while to make sure it was not my fault and to demonstrate I had done all I could. I am sorry for the times when I did not value others as much as You did. I am sorry for the times when I lost faith in Your continuous call even when the lost one has no plan to come home.*

*Lord, thank You for welcoming us home when we have had doubts and fears. Thank You for relentlessly looking for others. We find so much joy in celebrating returning brothers and sisters! We pray that we can see the wandering people as well as those stuck without any hope. We pray we can care for them as persons rather than just trying to "grow the church." Please unstop our ears and open our eyes so that we can more faithfully pray, "Thy kingdom come, Thy will be done."*

*In Jesus' name,*
*Amen*

---

Thank you for walking with me through Luke 15. Yes, I do have an eclectic taste in music. I hope that does not offend anyone. I am fond of jazz, oldies, classics, country, hymns, and other music forms that convey longings, hopes, dreams, failures, and faith. Perhaps music shares feelings of aloneness and lost hope in ways I can hear. Perhaps other art forms or parts of people's lives help you see where the lost can be found. I look forward to hearing about your next celebration—a celebration brought on by another person being welcomed by the Father. People of all walks of life deserve our welcome and celebration. No one has to ever walk alone.

God bless,

Jim

# 16 | A *WALK* THROUGH LUKE 16

Sometimes I wonder if pets and possessions own their masters or if the masters are in charge. One quickly learns that a nice car, house, pair of shoes, watch, or fountain pen needs care and maintenance if the owner expects the prized acquisition to stay in good condition. Any family that invites a cat, dog, or miniature pig into the house learns that the pet quickly runs the household and captures the affections of family members.

A few worldviews seek to detach from the "stuff" of life to find freedom. Western efforts to downsize possessions can be seen in the minimalist decorating styles. Eastern Buddhism seeks to distance self from as many things as possible. By detachment a person hopes to be free from suffering and all other aspects of life.

I do not think materialism limits itself to rich people. People in any station of life can be quite possessive of things and find a part of their identity in them. Jesus' teaching in the middle of Luke 16 addresses this basic truth: a person cannot serve both God and the stuff of life. While a few of His audience may have had possessions, most of them would have had little. Yet both rich and poor can spend their days acquiring and conserving stuff. Wars and unfair business practices take these personal behaviors to whole new levels.

Luke 16 provides another great example of Jesus' ability to convey wonderful truths through parables. His parables usually left the disinterested without understanding (Matthew 10:13–17). Those who wish to hear Jesus find themselves in the compelling stories. For those listeners, these two parables can perplex, convict, and point the way for faithful Kingdom living.

On the surface, Jesus seemed to advocate shrewd financial embezzlement when He said, "The children of this world are in their generation wiser than the children of light" (Luke 16:8). The wisdom zeroes in on one specific point. When the mismanaging steward gets kicked out of his position, he will find welcome in homes in the next period of his life. In his last days in office, he used what little power he had left to benefit others. In turn they would care for him.

The second parable goes straight to the rich man and bypasses the manager. He epitomizes the good life in his gated house, luxurious attire, and lavish dining. If he lived today, magazines would do pictorial spreads of his life. Reality TV shows would sign him to a contract so the "have-nots" could get lost in dreams about how it must feel to live like that. Of course, the magazines would skip the beggar pushing the dog away long enough to see if the garbage can held scraps from dinner.

Both parables convict the hearer. If one does not experience conviction, then that person did not hear. The good gifts I have come from the Father of lights (James 1:17). All the "stuff" that comes my way belongs to my Master since my baptism. Those who find a way to use those material gifts on behalf of others will find the afterlife a welcoming place. On the other hand, those who cannot faithfully use these trivial riches will not be trusted with true riches (Luke 16:11). Selfishly using the gifts in our hands exclusively for personal benefit (as the rich man did) horribly embezzles the Master's treasures. Luke's account calls me to prayer again.

*Dear Jesus,*

*Sometimes I do not want my ears to work. My under-standing of the "good life" looks so different from Yours! As I read Your parables again today, I must recommit to my choice to follow You. How quickly I return to self-centeredness when I go through times of blessings and times of suffering alike. I tend to treasure the things that come my way as something I have earned and deserve. I tend to doubt and question when suffering comes my way. Somehow I make both about me!*

*Forgive me, I pray. I live selfishly, and I live in a selfish nation. Forgive us, I pray. Open my ears again; I do want to hear how I can live more faithfully. All the Law and prophets came up to the time of John the Baptist. Those laws and prophecies do not pass away. They call us to walk boldly in the kingdom of God. Order my steps I pray. I think my mind and heart will have to be ordered before You can order my steps. For some reason, I sometimes think You will order my steps but will leave my self-centered mind and heart in place. My life is not a cartoon where I can be split into two or three dimensions. I must live completely in one dimension. I want that dimension to be in Your purposes.*

*Thank You for the wonderful gifts You have given Sherri and me! I know our many life opportunities came from You. I lift our lives up to You as a living sacrifice again today. Please purge away those things that reflect my selfish thinking. Help us to grow in ways that cause us to live for You and serve others.*

*In Jesus' name,*
*Amen*

Thank you for walking with me through Luke 16. Maybe reading these parables will cause you to pause and reflect on God's many good gifts in your life. Maybe we can all see more ways to bless others and reduce the scowls when we encounter someone in need. Maybe the Master let us be stewards of so much for moments like these. How blessed we are!

God bless,

Jim

# 17 | A *WALK* THROUGH LUKE 17

D r. Brauch, one of my old seminary professors (yes, he was old then, and that was nearly thirty years ago), wrote a book titled *The Hard Sayings of Paul*. It added to a series where various authors addressed difficult biblical passages. F. F. Bruce wrote the volume covering the sayings of Jesus. As I slowly read through Luke's gospel again, I wonder if any of Jesus' words could be excluded from a hard sayings book.

Some of Jesus' words may be hard to understand, but the real problem is how His words call for radical new life in the Kingdom. Jesus' birth, life, ministry, words, death, and resurrection all underscore this reality. If we could easily follow Jesus' words, then His death represented a wasteful slaughter. Jesus' hard sayings would fill volumes. Easy sayings might fit on a 3 x 5 notecard.

Reading Luke 17, I find the challenge in hearing Jesus places me in good company. Luke begins this section (yes, chapter headings came later, but the ordering of the stories goes back to Luke) with the reality of offending one another and the call to forgive. Offending a believer makes one eligible for a trip to the bottom of the sea in something that looks like a mobster's most recent hit. While offending makes us worthy of that end, the harder saying calls us to Jesus' brand of forgiveness.

His brand of forgiveness calls for confronting (or *carefronting* to borrow from another of my old professors) the offender so they can repent. If they repent, then you can forgive.

I think I would rather just forgive without the messiness of seeking restored relationship. Why not make it an easy saying by just forgiving without confronting to avoid the possibility of being rejected again? Why not get emotional freedom by just forgiving even if they don't want to repent? The disciples thought the same way. While they received Jesus' instructions to cast out demons in Luke 9 without a backward glance, the call to forgive the hard way caused them to cry out, "Lord, increase our faith!" (Luke 17:5).

Could it be that real spiritual warfare comes in confronting, repenting, and forgiving one another? Could it be that we exercise our faith in praying against devils because we do not have enough courageous faith to live in Jesus' kind of Kingdom relationships? I guess Jesus really did give hard sayings.

Jesus did not let up on the pressure. He said they [we] have enough faith to move trees. The problem was not the lack of faith; they already had enough faith. Jesus said the problem was obeying as servants should. Servants do not even earn rest after coming in from labor in the field; they start working on the master's dinner.

Kingdom living challenges me today. Kingdom living also frees me today. I cannot earn status with the Master, but I also do not have to understand why or how the Master's plans will come to pass. I am free to do the impractical with my life: follow the hard sayings of Jesus.

Success does not earn me status. Jesus' hard behaviors already provided the healing and wholeness. We see this in Luke 17 when a Samaritan ex-leper returned to glorify God. The stranger bowed when he saw the changes that came by walking in faith. He knew he would never get to see the priest as Jesus directed. His Jewish friends would have access to the priest, but he would be left on the outside looking in again. He received undeserved healing. He had to worship. Jesus piled wholeness on top of the healing. Kingdom living frees me from trying to earn wholeness. Kingdom living frees me to obey simply and joyfully.

Luke added some eschatology questions from the Pharisees to this series of narratives. They wanted to hear Jesus' prediction of when the kingdom of God would come. They participated in a whole cottage industry of kingdom-coming prognostication. Everyone had a guess. Everyone wanted to be the person who could tell others, "I told you so." They were like the futurist in the 1960s who just knew the work week would be down from forty to twenty-four hours and we would be flying around in personal car-planes by now. Instead Americans work longer hours than their predecessors from the past couple of generations and have the privilege of spending even more hours in traffic jams.

Jesus lovingly answered their question and continued the discussion with His disciples. The kingdom of God would not come with that kind of prognostication—a prognostication of how good everyone had to be for the Messiah to come and restore Israel's freedom. Instead the Kingdom was already among them! And they missed it. The Kingdom had already started and would eventually be completed in an unpredictable moment that would separate believers from unbelievers.

The only way I can learn this way of Kingdom living is by going to the Teacher in prayer.

---

*Dear Jesus,*
*I am free today, and I feel it. Thank You for Your sacrificial redemptive work that set me free. Thank you for helping me know I cannot earn this kind of loving relationship with You. I accept it in the faith You provide.*

*Forgive me for those times when I revert to the "easier" way of trying to prove I am good enough to be loved, that I deserve to be included. Forgive me for the times I resist Your hard sayings as impractical or impossible.*

*I realize I do not need more faith. I need to exercise the faith You have already placed in me and do those things You have lovingly commanded.*

*Thank You for welcoming strangers like me who come to worship. Thank You for the Kingdom that is already present and flourishing. I begin this day with anticipation of the ongoing expansion of the Kingdom. I look forward to serving as a Kingdom witness, as a Kingdom ambassador in a world in such need. We cry out together, "Master, have mercy on us!"*

*"Thy kingdom come, Thy will be done, in earth as it is in heaven."*

*In Jesus' name,*
*Amen*

---

Thank you for walking with me through Luke 17. Perhaps Jesus' hard sayings challenge you from time to time as well. Trust His wisdom and ways. Trust His work in you. Trust His promise that the Kingdom has already begun even though you do not yet see it completed. Trust Him by simply following His sayings rather than earning status on your own. Don't be afraid to confront, repent, and forgive.

God bless,

Jim

# 18 | A WALK THROUGH LUKE 18

Both the sciences and the humanities look for ways to understand how the world works. Perhaps the quest to unlock this mystery represents a significant part of what it means to be human. Animals have instincts; humans have questions.

Some psychologists of the twentieth century held a very mechanical view of human behavior. A few, like Pavlov and Skinner, thought human behavior could be understood by examining the conditioning and rewards people experience. Some of this holds true. We often learn that certain behaviors get rewards; saying thank you gets a pat on the head while saying no to Mom gets a little stronger pat on the bottom. Simple formulas, however, do not explain all human experience.

Luke 18 helps us see that faith does not follow simple formulas either. Jesus told one parable with the emphasis on praying always. The very next story shows the "good" guy who prays always goes away without God while the "bad" guy mumbles a cry for mercy. According to Jesus, the simple prayer transformed the second man into a justified state. At the end of the chapter a blind man only has a couple of sentences to say to Jesus, "Thou Son of David, have mercy on me," and "Lord, that I may receive my sight." Jesus responded to the simple request by giving the man even more than he asked. Jesus gave him sight and told him his faith saved him.

Should we pray always or not? Will God provide justice or send us home without relationship? Why pray always when two sentences can get such great results?

Other stories in the chapter examine a similar formula-busting phenomenon. Jesus' disciples pushed the children away. After all, if children can do very little, what would they add to the disciple group? Jesus rebuked such reasoning. Instead Jesus told the disciples the only way to receive the Kingdom was as a child! Those who had no value find an open door.

A rich ruler also came to Jesus. He wanted to know what he could *do* to inherit eternal life. Jesus set him up like a few teachers I know. He told the man to keep the commandments. The man affirmed he had already done that. Jesus then gave him the real answer, "Sell all you have, give to the poor, and follow me." The man left in deep sorrow. He could follow 613 Old Testament rules, but he could not take these three simple steps. He had too much wealth to just be a follower.

The disciples showed astonishment when they saw an obviously blessed person walk away. If a rich person could scarcely be saved, then what chance did they have?

Reading further I hear their perplexity give way to hope as Peter spoke for the team. While they were not wealthy like the rich guy, they had given up all and followed Jesus. Jesus quickly let them know they were on the right track. Giving up everything earned even more family now and in the age to come. Wow, we finally find the formula, the alchemy to transform mere human existence into eternal blessings!

Not so fast. Jesus had to tell the rest of the story, a story they would not understand.

Jesus chose this moment to give the prophecy-fulfilling agenda for the coming weeks: Jesus would be delivered to the Gentiles, mocked, spitefully used, spit on, scourged, and put to death. After three days, He would rise again.

Jesus had just told the disciples they would inherit rewards in this life and in the next. Now He tells them the One they had surrendered everything to follow would be put to death. We can almost see the "Does Not Compute" graphic pop in their minds. They banked everything on Jesus' success, and now He tells them He will voluntarily be shamed. Luke uses the words, "This saying was hid from them," to convey the impossible cognitive challenge before them (Luke 18:34). They would follow their Messiah to death rather than to a Joshua-like victory.

This journey will not fit a formula. This journey does call for prayer—sometimes long ones, sometimes short ones.

---

*Dear Jesus,*

*Sometimes I wish faith could be figured out. I wish someone could teach me the magic formula where I could pray the right way and at the right times for the exact outcome I seek. After all, I have tried to give up everything and follow You.*

*As I read Your Word, I realize such a formula would be a curse. Rather than building a relationship with You, where we as Your people commune with You in prayer, study of the Word, and serving others, we would just go to the proven formula. Formulas have no faith.*

*I must repent again. I am sorry for trying to figure out the magic formula. I am sorry for the times when I would prefer a wand over faith that rests in the unseen. I know my quest to understand it all stems from my fallen nature and an effort to control You and Your purposes. Forgive me, I pray.*

*I accept the call to carry this treasure in my earthen vessel. I accept the invitation to pray without ceasing in a way that hears Your voice and feels Your Spirit, rather than in a way that seeks my will to be done.*

*I receive Your blessings now. I also accept the reality of difficult places in the journey from here to there. I desire the touch You offered the children. I cry out with both the publican and the blind man, "Have mercy on me!" I accept healing of my eyes (and ears, I might add) that comes only through faith.*

*Thank You for not being a formula I can control. Such a formula would come from my limited perspective. Your grace would not be seen. I would miss the women who have no advocate, the children who go untouched, the faithful disciples who have given up more than I would ever know, and the beggars who are considered unworthy of an audience with You. Since my formulas are too small, I pledge to resist writing them.*

*"Thy kingdom come, Thy will be done." No other formula will work.*

*In Jesus' name,*
*Amen*

---

Thank you for walking with me through Luke 18. I hope the chapter helped you experience both the perplexity and absurdity of writing formulas that control God. Perhaps you will also find the courage to discard an outmoded formula or two as you seek to pray, give, receive healing, and suffer in accordance with the Word.

God bless,

Jim

# 19 | A *WALK* THROUGH LUKE 19

I have a confession to make. I enjoy elements of the Christian calendar. For me, the weeks leading up to Easter, Pentecost, and Christmas (Advent through Epiphany) should play a more critical role in the life of saints than holidays picked by Hallmark Cards or governmental bodies. While I value presidents, pilgrims, mothers, fathers, grandparents, laborers, and other people who have made significant contributions to our society, I like to examine the impact of Christian events on the calendar. I would probably trade Thanksgiving Day for All Saints Day (November 1). Rather than remembering early American settlers, I would choose to remember brothers and sisters who have gone on before us. I truly stand on giants' shoulders, and I am so thankful for their well-lived lives.

This year on Palm Sunday, North Point UPC in Sperry, Oklahoma, invited me to worship with them. I had the honor of preaching from Luke 19 in the morning service and from John 12's alabaster box story in the evening service. We encountered Jesus on our road to Easter as did that first generation of saints.

The journey from Jericho to Jerusalem was a short one, but the encounters provide tremendous insight into Jesus' desire to seek and save the lost (Luke 19:10). Each case reveals His desire to reach deeper than people's felt needs. Zacchaeus may have been short in stature, but he had a big reputation. As a rich tax collector, he evidently created many barriers between himself and his community. The walls protected him from their anger and suspicion. He climbed that tree by the road out of curiosity and looked over his protective wall to see Jesus. He did not go unnoticed.

Jesus went beyond Zacchaeus' felt need and exposed the deeper need. The taxman needed to let Jesus through his protective barriers. While a rich man in a previous chapter had to sell all of his possessions if he wanted to follow Jesus, Zacchaeus only had to let Jesus into his house for dinner. Salvation crossed the threshold. The other rich man's identity rested in his wealth. The rich taxman's identity existed in his isolation from God and neighbor. Once Jesus came in, the walls came down! Zacchaeus voluntarily gave away half of his wealth and conducted an audit to see if anyone would get a 400 percent tax rebate. The taxman got more than what he bargained for.

Meanwhile, the multitude looked for a messiah to cast out the Romans. Maybe this would be the Passover generations of Jews anticipated. Political and economic freedom would be theirs. They knew war would ensue, but the promised Messiah could handle it. They could have "peace in heaven, and glory in the highest" (Luke 19:38). Jesus entered the City of Peace as the Prince of Peace . . . the Prince of Peace now. Luke's Christmas story includes the angels' proclamation that peace had come to earth where good will would be to all humanity. Sadly the crowd failed to grasp the peace right in front of them as they sought release from a lesser bondage. Jesus wept again! Jerusalem's day had come, and the whole city missed it because they looked for the wrong things.

The crowd's momentary worship for anticipated freedom would require a future conflict. Misguided worship always does. The crowd turned from waving palm branches to waving fists and shouting insults within a week. Jesus just would not act right. Jesus would not meet their felt need.

Pharisees needed to control the mob—to be arbiters of orderly worship. They really needed to realize worship cannot be contained by human systems.

The priests needed to control religious practices for their own benefit. Jesus showed them the deeper need when He tipped over their tables. They had turned spiritual authority into a source of personal gain. They needed to return to praying for all nations.

In Oklahoma I got to preach the Word. I witnessed the Spirit and Word's impact on the gathered saints one more time. I prayed with folks and encouraged them to encounter Jesus. Then it happened—I encountered Jesus. My need for several weeks has revolved around a way to make this next period of ministry sustainable. I have asked Jesus how Sherri and I could support ourselves now that our work will not be centered in the familiar setting of the previous twenty-eight years. Jesus has given us peace now, but I still wonder how we will pay the bills.

I asked the audience to encounter Jesus; somehow I did not remember Jesus would hold me accountable to the Word as well. Jesus touched deep into my spirit. He knew my deeper need rested in seeing the value He places on my life and ministry now. He knew my deeper need revolved around knowing He has indeed called me to a valuable Kingdom work. He wanted me to know recentering around this truth was more important than worrying about July's house payment. Peace moved from Heaven to earth. I worshiped.

As I finish reading and reflecting on Jesus' journey to Jerusalem, I am called to prayer again.

*Dear Jesus,*

*I am so thankful You always push us to encounter You in a way that goes beyond our felt needs. I must confess and repent of those times I get frustrated and perplexed by Your focus on the deeper needs. I am sorry about my whining. I am sorry about putting my personal needs above Kingdom prayers for all nations. I am sorry for my lapses. I certainly need more table tipping. My prayers have drifted off target . . . again. They center more on what I need than on what the world needs.*

*Thank you for offering another encounter on Palm Sunday. You lovingly persisted and stripped away my defenses until I heard Your purposes. You pressed all of us for a deeper encounter with You than what we had planned. You are the gracious God! I thank You on behalf of a world that needs to see peace on earth as Your kingdom comes and Your will is done.*

*In Jesus' name,*
*Amen*

Thank you for walking with me through Luke 19. I know Jesus will push all of us for deeper encounters with Him. Maybe we can release our need and let Him do what He does best—remake us in His image. While you may be surprised by what Jesus changes deeply within you, you can trust Him to do all things well. Let's look forward to Horrendous Friday and Resurrection Sunday. Surely more encounters await us.

God bless,

Jim

# 20 | A *WALK* THROUGH LUKE 20

Some things never change. For quite a few years now nearly all social conversations relate to use and abuse of power. I once lived about seven miles from Ferguson, Missouri, a name that represents racial tension rather than a city itself. Anger burned hotter than the flames as the protests jumped from one small city in the midwestern US to metropolitan cities in the east. Media outlets filled the air with accounts, images, and despair. Urban death and violence continue.

In a sinful world people suffer in so many ways. Power abuse, victimization, rebellion, self-protection, and fear represent just a few of the ways society suffers as human beings harm self and each other. To bring order out of chaos, society endows some people and institutions with authority—the right to use power to make others conform. Small societies like families, churches, and gangs have their authority patterns as do cities, states, governments, stock markets, and multinational corporations. Change disrupts the balance and brings efforts to reassert some sense of order.

Some things never change. Luke 20 takes place during Passion Week as tensions heightened between Jesus and various authorities. This upstart Teacher had opened blind eyes, raised the dead, reinterpreted the Law, and tipped over Temple tables. Such behavior could not be tolerated. Something had to be done. Blind people belonged at their beggar's corner and low station in life. Dead people should stay put. The Law had to be explained by the right authorities. The Temple had a job to do, and chaos upset the economic, social, and religious balance.

Everyone talks about the weather, but no one does anything about it. Everyone talks about the pain of sin, but very few want anything to be done about it. This week has so much in common with that first Passion Week. By what right does Jesus mess up people's choices and consequences of those choices? Do we prefer sin's consequences to surrendering to Jesus' authority?

Luke 20 records heightened tensions where various influence groups questioned Jesus' authority. The power brokers could not question Jesus' power. He had proven His ability to attack brokenness and suffering too many times for them to deny His power. All they could question was His authority to use such disruptive power. Jesus engaged the various interrogators, but He would not answer their authority questions. He rejected their authority.

The parable did not help the court of public opinion. Jesus' story revealed how the fallen, sinful powers plotted to kill the Lord of the vineyard's heir. Jesus was that heir. He was the rejected stone. He had power and authority to confront all sources of abuse, even spiritual abuse. Since the fallen powers could not kill Jesus right after the palm-branch-strewn entry to Jerusalem, they set more traps to support a flimsy court case. They failed. They stopped questioning Jesus' authority.

The chapter ends with Jesus warning the crowd about the abusive power around them. Power abusers tried to generate authority by their robes, titles, and seats in the synagogues and at feasts. They siphoned off resources from the poor and glamorized themselves through lengthy prayers. Empty shells always fight to keep their ill-gotten authority. Some things never change by themselves; that is why I need to pray again.

*Dear Jesus,*

*I enjoy Easter's resurrection, but I do not know if I like Passion Week. Your work heightens the gap between Your authority and our efforts to keep control. Lord, You would think we would recognize instances when we work harder to protect our position than to actually use what little power we have to do righteousness.*

*Have mercy on me, I pray. How often have I challenged Your authority? Your power is beyond question. You have healed, saved, endowed with spiritual gifts, provided miraculously, and comforted in difficult times. Yet these days between Palm Sunday and Easter illustrate my feeble efforts to resist Your authority as Creator, Sustainer, and Redeemer. Have mercy on me, I pray.*

*Forgive me for times when my life pointed to my feeble power rather than Your divine authority. I pray Your Spirit guides Sherri and me in ways that we can point to Your goodness. Can we touch the sick, broken, marginalized, lonely, and dying as Your hands? All our resources are Yours; we pledged that in our baptism and reaffirmed it at our wedding. Instead of questioning Your authority, please help us serve as better farmers in the field.*

*All the abusive use of power in our world sickens You now as it did that first Passion Week. Sin has that effect on You. This Friday serves as a reminder of how much You hate sin and its effects on humanity and how far You go to break the power of sin. Thank You for Friday. I am sorry for my contribution to forging those nails.*

*Would You help me hear the warning You gave the audience at the end of the chapter? Too often I accept the broken world as "just the way things are." Your passion rejects my acceptance. I need spiritual strength to confront the weakened powers of this world. The fallen systems*

*work so hard to keep their power—power You unmasked
and broke on Calvary's hill. Sometimes I fail to see how
I benefit from the brokenness of the world. Forgive me
and open my eyes to what You see. I give up my "piece
of the action" in abusive power. All lives matter, particularly those who suffer at the expense of abusive power in
a broken world.*

*Thank You for unmasking the shame of power abuse by
Your suffering. Every time You expose power abuse, I see
Your kingdom coming and Your will being done.*

*In Jesus' name,*

*Amen*

---

Thank you for walking with me through Luke 20. I
realize my devotions sound a little political today, but reading
about Jesus' Passion Week shines a light on sin wherever it
may be. I pray you have a powerfully redeeming week as you
look forward to Friday and Easter.

God bless,

Jim

# 21 | A *WALK* THROUGH LUKE 21

Several years ago one of my UGST (Urshan Graduate School of Theology) colleagues and I had the privilege of teaching Bible college instructors in an African capital city. I was humbled by the lives of service, faith, and endurance represented by the men in the room. I will never forget my time with them. I am sure I learned more from them than they did from me.

A bonus treat of such trips so far from home is the chance to see things I've only read about. Of course most of my travel was at thirty-five thousand feet rather than more intimate travel by ship, train, bus, and camel. Flying can be a little frustrating even though it saves weeks or months in the journey. For example, the pilot announced we could see the pyramids out of the left side of the plane. I was within six miles (straight up) of the pyramids, but could not see them because I was on the wrong side of the plane. A little while later, I sat with my fellow travelers on the Alexandria, Egypt, tarmac. Oh how I wanted to get out and see where one of the world's ancient libraries stood and where the Lighthouse of Alexandria once stood! I had missed the sites of two of the seven ancient wonders of the world that day. One was the pyramids—the only survivor of the ancient list of human achievements. The other was the site of the lighthouse that surrendered to an earthquake seventeen hundred years after its construction.

85

As I walk through Luke 21, I am transported back to old Jerusalem. I can hear the clamor in the streets as the population swelled to accommodate Passover pilgrims from all over the known world. The smells of all the cattle waiting to be sacrificed would have far eclipsed my fresh country air childhood experiences in upstate New York dairy country. A little, insignificant-looking man led a small gaggle of students on a field trip to the Temple. It could easily belong on the Seven Wonders of the Ancient World list along with the Temple of Artemis in Ephesus or the Statue of Zeus at Olympia.

How refreshing it would be to see ancient sites where people experienced what they saw rather than viewing the world through a cell phone camara. Rather than capturing selfies, everyone was pointing out notable points of interest. Herod had begun to rebuild and expand the Temple in 20 BC, and the project would not be finished until about thirty years after the events recorded in Luke 21. So many beautiful stones and gold embellishments covered the Temple. Many art objects came from generous donations of wealthy worshipers.

The Teacher didn't follow with the normal assessment of things. He rarely did. When comparing the loud clang of wealthy givers to the tinkle of the widow's two mites, the strange Thinker said she gave more than the rich; she gave all she had.

The unruly students did what I have experienced when I led field trips in my elementary school teaching days—they pointed out different things from the teacher. They looked at the permanence of the structure and wondered at the beauty of the huge stones. Their Teacher said every stone would be brought down very soon. Now He had their attention! The collective ethnic psyche remembered the last time the Temple came down roughly six hundred years before.

Jesus had a teachable moment.

False christs, wars, earthquakes, famine, pestilence, and fearful sights in the heavens would be precursors of the destruction. Disciples would need to prepare themselves for rejection from society, friends, and family. But once again the Teacher gave a twist to the normal understanding of unfair court trials. What was meant to intimidate and shame would be turned into a witnessing opportunity where the Spirit would gift them with the right words to say. With patience they would endure the civil crises.

They would also know to flee the city when army camps gathered around. They should flee the city before God's judgment came at the hands of Roman legions. Josephus gave estimates of a death toll of one million and as many as ninety-seven thousand captives taken from the city. Genocide came with the destroyed beauty.

Jesus extended the teachable moment to talk about His return in the clouds.

As assuredly as the Teacher wanted the disciples to be forewarned of Roman scorched-earth tactics, He needed future generations of followers to stay ready for the Son of Man's return with full power. Jerusalem would not be ready and would not survive the Roman slaughter. Would future disciples fare any better? When the whole cosmos suffered as Jerusalem's environs fell in AD 70, would saints be watching? Or would they "be overcharged with surfeiting, and drunkenness, and cares of this life, and so that day come upon you unawares" (Luke 21:34)?

How can I read Luke 21 without answering the call to watch and pray?

---

*Lord Jesus,*

*I covet to see circumstances as You see them. I know this request comes with much upheaval in my spirit. Places where I think I have given so much may actually turn out to be so little. Places where I was ashamed that I had so little to give may be a high point of worship. In settings where I see stability and beauty, You often see decay and judgment. I must add the need for wisdom and the peace of the Spirit to my request to see, or I will not be able to handle what You show me.*

*I throw my two pennies in Your heavenly treasury today. Prepare me with patience for the days and the witnessing opportunities that are to come. Help me to realize I do not walk this path alone. I need brothers and sisters who quest to understand the seasons and give no place for the cares of this life. Together we can reject these cares in favor of the Kingdom's fulfillment when You come in the clouds. What a day that will be to stand before You! Surely, we can surrender to the Spirit's leading, live faithfully until the end, and be ready to hear, "Well done." Until that day we will focus our prayer on Thy kingdom come and Thy will be done.*

*In Jesus' name,*
*Amen*

---

Thank you for walking through Luke 21 with me. The horrors of Jerusalem's destruction and pending global conflagration give us pause to consider our readiness for Christ's return. I believe we can look forward with hope and blessing rather than fear if we only have eyes to see and ears to hear.

God bless,
Jim

# 22 | A *WALK* THROUGH LUKE 22

Fifty of my sixty years of life have been spent in school. Some years I was a student. Some years I was the teacher. About half of the time, I found myself balancing the two sides of the desk—I submitted papers in some classrooms and graded papers from others in my classroom. A major concern for my academic life, from kindergarten in Galatia, Illinois, to the vice president and professor at UGST in Florissant, Missouri, was the need for academic integrity. According to the International Center for Academic Integrity, as many as 60 percent of university students admit to engaging in some form of cheating.

Current trends in education lean toward helping students live out core values rather than simply focusing on wrong behaviors to be avoided. The International Center for Academic Integrity identifies six core values that schools at all levels can follow to foster an environment of integrity where learning can take place: honesty, trust, fairness, respect, responsibility, and courage. Surely maturing in those core values would maximize learning more than values of competition, getting ahead regardless of the cost, earning status, and finding shortcuts when life gets difficult. I guess I am still a recovering professor; writing like this makes me feel nostalgic for the classroom even though it would mean helping students know how to apply proper citations in their research papers.

As I walk through Luke 22, I am broken by failures of integrity. Every character, except Jesus, seems to violate the most basic understandings of integrity. Each paragraph reeks of failed opportunities to live in accordance with values that people profess to follow. Perhaps Parker Palmer's hypothesis in his classic work, *Courage to Teach,* is correct: fear is the greatest inhibitor to teaching and learning.

Here are integrity failures I see in the chapter:

- Judas asked the chief priests and captains about the best way to betray Jesus. Judas was not the only one with failed integrity in verse 3.

- The disciples sought to be the greatest when their Teacher lived to be a servant of all.

- The disciples failed to practice prayer in hours of temptation though Jesus pointed out the need and modeled it Himself.

- Simon Peter would deny even knowing Jesus after protesting his faithfulness in no uncertain terms.

- The high priest's servants spoke blasphemy.

- The Sanhedrin council members, a collective of religious leaders from across Jewish society, interrogated Jesus without the least interest in learning the truth.

Evidently the pressures of Kingdom reversal demands were greater than people's professed core values. Where the disciples once experienced open arms of hospitality as they cast out demons, healed the sick, and preached the Kingdom, they now heard Jesus speak of unsafe conditions in front of them. They mistook the words about swords as a call to violence, woefully inept violence at that, rather than a metaphor for the opposition they would face. At least their failure gave an opportunity for Jesus to model nonviolence and loving enemies when He healed the high priest's servant's ear with a simple touch (Luke 22:51). Jesus was telling the disciples, in essence, "That is enough."

Even as I reflect on Luke 22, I must echo Isaiah's words, "Woe is me!"

The above exclamation explodes from my soul as I move into the scene where Jesus reclined at the table and the disciples followed. He had waited for this last holy meal since He began calling the disciples back in chapter five. All twelve disciples had their hands on the table. Jesus shared the bread and cup that represented His body and blood: the bread of remembrance and the cup of the New Testament in His blood. The table powerfully revealed betraying and strife. Jesus divided the bread, and they argued about who could be a master like the Gentiles.

Woe is me! As I smell the broken bread and catch a whiff of the passing cup, weaknesses in my spiritual integrity get exposed. This exposure is an act of Jesus' amazing grace! The exposure gives me no option but to grab the opportunity to pray.

---

*Lord Jesus,*

*I marvel at Your love for all Your disciples! As we carry this treasure in earthen vessels, we discover more and more places where we do not fully measure up to Your kingdom principles. As disciples we suffer weaknesses in our integrity, yet You patiently love and call us again anyway.*

*I repent of interloping wrong values. I repent of competition and the need to be in charge. I accept the Kingdom values of faith, hope, and love. I eat of the bread and drink of the cup with fellow disciples as we commit to maturing in You. Unlike the first Twelve, we know how the next few chapters unfold. We know You paid the ultimate price for us to live out the Kingdom rather than our old ways. We know You resurrected and sent Your Spirit so that we could live on Your mission rather than our self-interest.*

*I find great delight in praying, "Thy kingdom come, Thy will be done!" The prayer calls me and my fellow worshipers back to spiritual integrity and holiness one more time. You invest us with purpose, power, and passion as we do so.*

*In Jesus' name,*
*Amen*

---

Thank you for walking with me through Luke 22. The chapter will always present a challenge as we find ourselves at the table and asleep in the garden. We grieve and give thanks at the same time when we think about Jesus' trial on our behalf. The chapter also gives us hope as we eat the bread and drink the cup together. Maybe we will have a chance to do that down here someday. If not, we will eat it with Him at the Table over there.

God bless,
Jim

# 23 | A *WALK* THROUGH LUKE 23

On this Friday morning I sit at the airport waiting for my Easter trip to New Jersey. Everything looks so normal. People drink Starbucks coffee and check their text messages. Families shepherd their little children and hope to board early. People keep their two bags within arm's reach. The airport version of CNN tells the news of a Walmart employee getting fired for some strange reason, and the abused United Airlines traveler's lawyers position themselves for a hefty payout. The day looks normal for travelers and workers alike.

But today is not a normal Friday. Today *is that* Friday—the Friday when everything changed.

Change presents challenges. Universities offer degrees in change management. Laws of physics as well as family systems theory remind us that natural forces resist change. Cool words like equilibrium and homeostasis provide labels for this phenomenon. Unchecked change would bring everything we know to a state of complete chaos.

But on Good Friday we remember everything did change. Chaos still comes with the Cross.

Perhaps you have heard people introduce a new dish, art form, or music genre by saying, "You will either really like it, or you will hate it." The Cross had the same effect. Luke 23 demonstrates the way the Cross clarifies what is on the inside of a person. While Pilate tried to escape responsibility of Jesus' trial, he became good friends with his old enemy Herod by rejecting Jesus. Most of the crowd who had paraded for Jesus a few days before now asked for Barabbas's release. Since Jesus would not be their kind of king, they would prefer an anarchist and murderer. Soldiers mocked the rival Jewish king who could be put to death so easily.

The two thieves demonstrate the dividing nature of the Cross. One malefactor ridiculed Jesus and betrayed the evil of his heart. The other felon somehow observed the difference between himself and Jesus. He deserved to die; Jesus did not. In fact, no one else in the chapter confessed Jesus was still King and would inherit His kingdom soon. The spiritually sensitive outcast asked to be remembered when Jesus achieved His goal.

Some of Jesus' old crowd still followed in an anticipatory funeral procession. They wept for Jesus. The condemned Savior suggested they weep for themselves. Society's response to Jesus, a righteous man, demonstrated they too would be mistreated. A few of those devout followers from Galilee would continue to follow even after Jesus' admonition. Simon probably had blood transfer to his robe when the soldiers conscripted him to carry the cross, but these few faithful believers might have stayed close enough to have the blood splatter on them as well. They would even follow Joseph, the minority counselor who voted for acquittal, to observe where Jesus' body would rest. They went home to prepare more spices to worship Jesus once the Sabbath had ended.

The heavens mourned, and the earth quaked. Darkness fell, and the veil ripped. That Friday changed everything.

Luke 23 does not provide a Hollywood-worthy script. The agony of Christ does not get enough attention for bloodthirsty moviegoers. Luke limited descriptions of Jesus' pain to just a few sentences. He preferred to capture the impact of the Cross on others. After all, could anyone really describe the horror of that day? Perhaps the three-hour total eclipse alone could tell the magnitude of what happened.

Luke did illuminate Jesus' response to those around Him. Not only did He invite the thief to stay by His side forever, He interceded on behalf of those who carried out the government's order and the mob's will. They may have ridiculed and gambled for His garments, but He would spend His remaining agonizing breaths in prayer for them.

When He could hold on no longer, Jesus commended His spirit to the Father's hands. That Friday changed everything and still calls me to prayer.

---

*Dear Jesus,*

*My words seem so insignificant compared to Your sacrifice. You despised the shame and endured Your cross for the joy set before You. "Thank you" may be appropriate for a birthday gift or a meal in a friend's home, but the words fall short today.*

*Forgive me for the times I have so abruptly changed from joyfully following You to angrily thinking or feeling that You were not acting very king-like. Too often I see my own scowl, frown, fear, or disappointment in the mob. You only walked with them for three years or so; this summer I celebrate fifty years of Your Spirit abiding in me. Have mercy, I pray.*

*Remind me again how that Friday changed everything. Remind me of the ways the Cross separates people based on what they are on the inside. I have often stayed on the right side of the Cross. Please consume anything that would pull me away from Your side. Surely the Cross still has the power to invite thieves into Your eternal presence. I find too much thievery in me. Too often I have tried to use Your gifts for myself rather than to help serve others like You taught us to do.*

*While You still welcome thieves, I want to be transformed into the kind of disciple those women represented. I want to follow always. I want to observe where You are always. I want to worship always. I want to find rest even in challenging moments as they did. Dear Lord, make this Friday the day that changes me.*

*"Thy kingdom come, Thy will be done."*

*In Jesus' name,*

*Amen*

---

Thank you for walking with me through Luke 23. My devotions today are not worthy to be compared with the Crucifixion story, but I feel welcomed in the reality of this Friday nonetheless. Perhaps you find areas in your life that fall on both sides of the Cross divide as I did today. I pray you have the strength to cry out with the rest of us thieves. The Cross can make a difference in us today. The Cross calls us, reclaims us, and commissions us to live out the coming resurrection.

God bless,

Jim

# 24 | A *WALK* THROUGH LUKE 24

Who wants to know the truth? Who can handle the truth? Everywhere I turn these days folks want to know if anyone wants to know the truth anymore. Media outlets seem to go back to yellow journalism of the early twentieth century. Politicians point their fingers at opponents as people who refuse to face the truth or are so foolish they cannot even know the truth when it hits them between the eyes.

Jesus' followers often say postmodern people do not want to know the truth.

This quest for truth goes back a very long way! John recorded a conversation between Pilate and Jesus. The administrator asked Jesus, "What is truth?" Sadly he did not sit down and wait for an answer. He suffered from the ability to ask questions without the patience to listen for an answer.

Human beings seek to make meaning in life. We need to find a way to explain things that go on around us. We often make the same mistake Pilate did—we do not wait to hear Jesus explain the meaning of truth. Jesus wants to explain the whole truth. Can we handle the whole truth? Jesus proclaimed He is the Way, the Truth, and the Life. Jesus alone is doctrinal truth (also known as orthodoxy). All other truth systems get evaluated by Him. Jesus alone is truth in action or behavior (also known as orthopraxy). Everyone's actions will be measured against His action. Jesus is also the only measure of emotional, volitional, or inner-person truth (also known as orthopathy). Human will, motivations, and emotions must be conformed to Jesus.

Luke 24 proclaims so much truth, all three aspects of truth. Jesus resurrected from the tomb after having suffered to provide access for others to enter His glory (Luke 24:25–26). Jesus "opened . . . their understanding, that they might understand the scriptures" (Luke 24:45). Jesus spoke truth, doctrinal truth that confronted misunderstandings from the past.

Luke ended the chapter with concrete action items for those who would accept the truth of who He was. They had truth to *do* just as they had truth to *know*. They would preach the power of His name among all nations. They would take His whole message and actions into every nation. Truth in action takes the gospel to literally all people. Doing truth requires power, Holy Spirit power, that would come to them in Jerusalem. Disciples became doers of truth because of the teaching, life, death, and resurrection of Jesus.

Luke spent significant effort in capturing the emotional and motivational elements of truth in chapter 24.

- The women had perplexity in their emotions. They had labored all night to grind the spices for Jesus' decaying body, but the tomb was empty.

- When the women saw the two angels, they experienced fear.

- Peter and the others thought the women spoke idle tales. They could not receive the truth of their words because of the lack of truth in their spirit and emotions. Peter's emotional state drove him to look for himself. Luke mapped Peter's emotional journey from unbelief to confused wonder.

- The two Emmaus Road travelers tried to satisfy themselves with the factual kind of truth. They reasoned among themselves. Their reasoning left them emotionally out of balance. Jesus directly addressed their lack of emotional truth when He asked why they were sad.

- The two men told their story. Emotional struggles can be found in their sense of betrayal. He would not be the kind of messiah they wanted. He would not restore Israel as a nation. Their broken emotional truth related to their erroneous doctrinal truth.

- They confessed emotional astonishment at the women's testimony.

- Jesus evaluated their degree of emotional truth. They were "slow of heart to believe all that the prophets have spoken" (Luke 24:25). The problem centered in emotional truth rather than in doctrinal truth. Jesus explained Moses' and the prophets' doctrinal truth, but they still did not see Jesus for who He was.

- When the Emmaus travelers offered the Stranger customary hospitality, they finally had an opportunity to know truth. As Jesus received, blessed, broke, and gave the bread, they received truth. Jesus did not need to hang around anymore. The burning in their hearts matured to the place of truth. Their emotional truth transformation compelled them to run the seven and a half miles back to Jerusalem to witness the Resurrection truths (all three truths: truth in the event, truth in emotions, and truth in witnessing after seeing Jesus).

- Jesus showed up. Jesus' words addressed their lack of emotional truth when He said, "Peace be unto you" (Luke 24:36). Luke explained they felt terror and fear in their spirit.

- Jesus questioned their emotional turmoil: "Why do thoughts arise in your hearts?" (Luke 24:38). Even touching Jesus did not put truth in their emotions. They could not believe. They could not accept the joy Jesus offered.

- After eating with Jesus, the disciples would finally receive emotional truth and believe Jesus. Consequently they worshiped and returned to Jerusalem with great joy even though He had parted from them.

I wish the emotional, behavioral, and doctrinal truth problems ended with the first-century disciples. Since I still see incomplete fulfillment of truth in my own life, I need to pray in light of Luke 24.

---

*Dear Jesus,*

*Thank You for all Resurrection truths! I had such a blessed Easter with the church family in Wrightstown, New Jersey, this year. Easter confronts me with Resurrection knowledge. The empty tomb calls me to live in authority and power of the Holy Spirit as I witness to Your goodness to all nations. This Easter, however, I must confess that my emotions, spirit, and motivations need to be transformed by truth.*

*I confess I still have moments of perplexity, fear, confusion, distrust, sadness, and absence of peace. Tasting Your meal, hearing Your words, and feeling Your presence brings deeper truth to my spirit. My labor shifts from obligation to the wonderful joy of being about Your work in the world. Easter calls me to reveal my inner weakness to You and to some other people around me. When my emotions stand in Your resurrection truth, I face the choice to believe and rejoice in the Resurrection or cherish fear and distrust.*

*Thank you for bringing truth to me in all dimensions this Easter season. Thank you for pushing beyond my natural tendency to protect my inner being from the possibility of hope . . . a possibility I resist for fear of yet another shattered dream. Easter calls me to trust. Easter calls me to accept the possibility that the world around me really does want to know truth—the whole truth.*

*"Thy kingdom come, Thy will be done."*

*In Jesus' name,*

*Amen*

---

Thank you for walking with me through Luke 24 in Easter's aftermath. Perhaps these days following the celebration you will have an opportunity to examine the degree of truth in your inner being. Please join with me in trusting Jesus afresh. Please join with me in breathing deeply from Easter's peace and joy!

God bless,

Jim

# 25 | A *WALK* THROUGH ACTS 1

I guess I am a little jaundiced when it comes to product promises that sound too good to be true. Some advertising firms still advise their clients to roll out the unbelievable product or deal to be coming soon. Perhaps such grand, veiled, hype-inducing pledges still work with other people, but they do not even get my attention anymore. Promises of a new iPhone or other gadget get people to attend unveiling conferences and stand in line all night to get the new product. I do not even click the links anymore.

I just do not quite get it, but then again, I was still using an iPhone 4 when someone convinced me I needed an iPhone 10. The old one still made and received calls, kept my calendar, and could even take pictures. (I think the digital camera roll had at least twenty pictures on it.) I think the only thing that would get me to stay up past 10:30 PM to hear new Apple product information would be that the greatest phone ever would be available for free with no plans to develop a next version since this one could not be improved. That promise might get my attention. I am not holding my breath.

Reading Acts 1 makes me feel like a new product rollout will happen soon. Luke continued the saga of all that Jesus did and taught in this second volume. He made it sound like the gospel actually continued. The blowing of the Spirit continued right where he left off. Jesus had given His apostles commandments by the Spirit. The coming promise of the Spirit would greatly exceed John's water baptism. The Spirit would bring power to witness from their home territory to the ends of the earth. This same Spirit that worked in David as he prophesied would play a significant role in part two of the gospel.

What brand-new promise would Jesus introduce? He had just died and resurrected. He had spent forty glorious days with the disciples (a drastically different forty days than His forty days of testing) where He showed infallible truths and talked about the kingdom of God. One would think the old Jesus was back in full force! And now He promised a new product rollout. Jesus would have had my attention along with the others.

Jesus' words and deeds require a response. Acts 1 illustrates this principle. With the pending new thing, the faithful wanted more information: "Lord, wilt thou at this time restore again the kingdom to Israel?" (Acts 1:6).

Somehow Jesus did not roll His eyes like technophiles do when they see my vintage cell phone. Instead Jesus lovingly redirected their hopes and curiosity. Jesus simply told them it was not for them to know the times or the seasons. Then the Master pointed their attention to a more significant question. The better question would have been, "Lord, how do we continue to do Your work after You are gone? How will we be able to do this without You?"

Jesus answered the unasked question, "Ye shall receive power after that the Holy Ghost is come upon you: and ye shall be witnesses unto me both in Jerusalem, and in all Judea, and in Samaria, and unto the uttermost part of the earth" (Acts 1:8). His answer revealed how drastically they missed the brand-new opportunity before them. The "product" upgrade exceeded their ability to dream. Their kind of kingdom with their ethnic and geographical limits did not fit the new product any more than the telegraph can compare to the newest do-everything-iPhone about to be released.

Jesus' new product prepared His people to go in authority and power to witness the Kingdom.

No wonder they did not get it.

They did what they could. They spent time in prayer and supplication. They practiced problem-solving and held business meetings. Perhaps equally important was their ability to abide in one accord.

They waited until the new product came and they could get it. As I read of their inability to fully grasp Jesus' new thing in them, I realize I need to pray for greater openness to His new work in my world today.

---

*Dear Jesus,*

*Luke's introductory chapter just blew my mind! I do not know how else to say it. Your departure included the wonder of new possibilities for Kingdom living and Kingdom witnessing. Somehow You gave them, as well as us today, such an unbelievable promise even when we ask bad questions. You actually invite us to be a part of Your work in reconciling the whole world to Yourself. Unbelievable!*

*Lord, forgive me of small thinking and small questioning. Like the original band of followers, I often think I am asking for a new, grand, Kingdom-coming reality when I am really looking in the wrong direction.*

*Oh Lord, could You speak to us, Your people, one more time? Reading Your Word in the authority of the Holy Spirit, I believe You want to gift us and send us in places beyond our wildest imagination. As You forgive our bad questions, give us the right answers, I pray.*

*Lord, could You unite us in prayer and supplication? Could You rebuke us of divisions, pride, competition, and clamoring for positions? Could You teach us to problem-solve in ways that anticipate the Kingdom's new work for this season?*

*I know these questions are too small, so I invite better answers than my questions deserve.*

*"Thy kingdom come, Thy will be done."*

*In Jesus' name,*

*Amen*

---

Thank you for walking with me through Acts 1. Perhaps you will join me in anticipating God's big kingdom rollout for our world today. I think our questions have been too small. Forgive me if I have ever harmed you in any way. Please let me know so I can get rid of those things in me that inhibit the one-accordness needed for the Next Big Thing waiting room.

God bless,

Jim

# 26 | A *WALK* THROUGH ACTS 2

According to my mother, I began my career as a researcher quite early in life. One of my favorite early childhood words was *why*. Evidently I used this key quest to gather data about the natural world ("Why is the grass green?") as well as human relationships ("Why do I have to do that?"). If my young mind did not find satisfaction, then I would ask a follow-up question. Apparently Mom nurtured, or at least tolerated, my questioning orientation toward life, for I continued to ask why questions through my years of formal education and my professional life.

As a professor I learned the value of a good question. I think a good question often held more transformative power than an hour-long lecture. Of course, I held my students to a high standard of questions as well. Though not always appreciated, I never subscribed to the there-are-no-bad-questions philosophy of life. I have heard some bad questions. Sadly, bad questions can generate bad or even dangerous answers.

I often try to get people to ask good questions after they read a portion of Scripture. Whether they read a paragraph, multiple chapters, or an entire book of the Bible, disciples should always ask a few questions. What did I learn? How can I live out this understanding? How can I change my prayers to be more in line with the Word?

I find some great questions in Acts 2. After observing the new Pentecostal phenomenon, many of the devout pilgrims who clogged Jerusalem's streets asked, "What meaneth this?" (Acts 2:12). Of course, others chose to mock rather than ask questions. They tried to explain the phenomenon by foolishly accusing the newly Spirit-filled followers of Christ of being drunk on cheap wine. The good questioners, and some of the mockers, responded to Peter's sermon with another great question, "What shall we do?" (Acts 2:37). In fact, Peter's sermon seems to end with a creative tension in the air. The crowd had to ask the good question before they got the opportunity to join in the new Pentecostal experience.

I have heard many people weaken the question from Acts 2:37 down through the years. Perhaps due to our Pentecostal tradition, many saints add " . . . to be saved" to the end of the question. These three additional words bleed off much of the power of the original question. The addition limits the original question to a terminal condition of being saved. The revised question also keeps people from continuing to ask this critical question after they have been saved.

Hearing the message of Jesus and the early church's response in Acts 2 calls me to ask the better question this morning, "What should I do?" I still ask this question even though I celebrate my fiftieth anniversary of Spirit infilling later this summer. The weaker, longer question blocks my ears from hearing what the Spirit says today. The weaker, longer question blocks my heart from responding to the convicting words of the passage. The weaker, longer question shortens my arms' reach to the threshold responses rather than the life-long claim of the Spirit's indwelling.

What should I do . . .

- about the power of Pentecost?

- about the devout people around me that observe the Spirit's work?
- about questioners and mockers?
- about the offering of visions, dreams, and prophecies—an offering that seems strangely underclaimed today?
- about the limits of those gifts to just a few when the sermon opens it to all flesh?
- about ways I limit all flesh just as Peter would in Acts 10?
- about the signs of pending judgment?
- about the tendency to limit the power of the Spirit to gathered worship where so few devout and mocking people can see it in public spaces?
- about the "far off" people that still have not heard this message?
- about the "untoward generation" elements that can still be found in me?
- about the full breadth of the new Pentecostal liturgy (continuing in the Apostles' doctrine, fellowship, breaking of bread, prayers, sharing resources as a loving and living witness, praying with others in public spaces, going from house to house, eating with gladness and singleness of heart, and praising God)?
- about finding favor with people in the world?
- about seeing the Lord's daily addition plan?

There I go again . . . so many questions. Some of them undoubtedly reach a higher level of questioning than others, but all of them come alive with the original Act 2:37 question. New hearers and old hearers alike can zero in on one or two of the questions for a season. As long as we stay repented and in our baptism, the infilling of the Spirit will lead us in the Lord's new Pentecostal purposes.

These questions call me to prayer.

---

*Dear Lord,*

*I repent again. I have dropped off on my questioning these past few months as I dealt with some other life situations. Your Word calls me to hear and ask better questions. I stay in my baptism—a baptism that commits to my rejection of old creaturely ways—to live in Your resurrection and actively participate in Your body.*

*Lead on, Holy Spirit. Help me see which of my questions should guide me at this time. Help me to persistently pursue good answers for my mind, my heart, and my actions. Help me to live them out in the original Oneness unity liturgy of that first Pentecost. Help me to ask questions that remind me that the answers only come as I pray, "Thy kingdom come Thy will be done."*

*In Jesus' name,*

*Amen*

---

Thank you for walking with me through Acts 2. I trust the walk generates some new questions for you to pursue as well. Perhaps some of my questions will help you think about the new Pentecostal liturgy in this powerful chapter.

God bless,

Jim

# 27 | A *WALK* THROUGH ACTS 3

My brothers and I continually received the benefit of loving parents. In their later years we got to hear many stories from their childhood. We grew up with some of these stories like a favorite blanket or stuffed animal—something that becomes a part of who you are even if the blanket becomes frayed or the bear only looks through one eye. I wonder why disabilities in a favorite toy does not scare us like those we find in the lives of our neighbors. Perhaps we can learn to love the suffering neighbor, possibly even feeling lost without neighbors, as much as we love the things that we cherish so much.

One story from Dad's childhood relates to Bill, one of his schoolmates. Dad had the privilege of attending a one-room schoolhouse that nurtured pupils from first through eighth grades. Dad and the other graduating eighth grader hold the honor of being the last to complete grammar school in the hallowed room. The institution carried the heavy moniker of Hale's College. Reverend Hale could not support his higher education dream in southern Missouri farm country, so he settled for a foundational education institution instead.

Bill may have suffered from anemia as well as poverty. As late autumn turned cold under the encroachment of Old Man Winter, Bill would add another layer of clothing. Each pair of pants would need to be a little larger than the previous pair to provide mobility while holding out the frost. Bill, like many little boys, liked to fill his pockets with found things. I doubt any of the items retained their shine; time marked them before they found a place in Bill's possession.

Bill's essential wardrobe did provide one advantage—for a finder. Each layer of pants afforded four more pockets, and by spring, all sixteen of them were filled with treasures! With so much on a little fellow's mind, he could not keep an accurate inventory of his holdings. One day Mr. Stafford, hopefully Dad's favorite teacher since he studied under that professor's tutelage for seven of his eight grammar school years, suffered the loss of a castor on his chair.

He called Bill to the teacher's desk.

"Bill, would you happen to have one of these little wheels in your pocket?" inquired the professor.

"I don't know," confessed the shy little scholar. He commenced to search through his inventory, one layer of pockets at a time. I must confess this is one time I wish phone video cameras existed in the late 1940s and early 1950s. What treasures like bent nails, broken watches, bullet casings, and shiny rocks must have emerged from the protective layers!

"Will this one work, Sir?"

"Bill, I believe you have done it!" exclaimed the teacher as he installed the castor and beamed on the lad who had already begun filling his spring pants pockets on the way to the winter stratum.

The lame beggar at Gate Beautiful undoubtedly looked at Peter and John with a similar expectation as Mr. Stafford bestowed on Bill. Would these young men be able to hold off hunger for him and his family for another day? Might he even face the coming Sabbath's forced rest with enough to sustain them until the next week without an unscheduled fast day? The apostles had empty pockets just like the last forty times they passed him on the way to prayer. They had even passed the same beggar with their Rabbi on His trips to the Temple. But this day proved to be different.

Empty pockets blessed the lame man.

He received something far greater as the men spoke the name of Jesus into the situation. He walked. He ran. He jumped. He beheld Peter and John as equal men rather than a beggar more familiar with worn knees than smiling eyes.

He praised God, and so did the people!

The people also displayed wonder and amazement. And Peter had the audacity to ask them why. I think they marveled justly—certainly more justly than the fact that Bill had come across the correct size castor in the previous four months and preserved it until his professor had a need.

The lame man's gift did not come from Peter and John's power or holiness (hmm, I could write a little about the beauty of holiness here, but that will have to be another story). The man did not experience restoration to health for he was lame from his mother's womb. Instead he experienced something never known before when faith in the name of the Prince of Life breathed across the courtyard.

Wonder of wonders! This time of refreshing comes from the presence of the Lord. These refreshing waves start with repentance and will continue until all creation's sinful brokenness gets restored. The healed limbs pointed to the coming destination. I should not camp at the sign or I will never make it to the destination.

Moses and the prophets spoke of this new possibility. A possibility where healing, repentance, restoration, blessings for all ethnic groups, and turning from all iniquities would become normal.

I still marvel when this happens, and it still calls me to pray.

*Dear Jesus,*

*I'm sorry. I want to turn to the signs rather than in the direction You intend for my life as I become part of the great restoration of all things. Too often I marvel and wonder when You do the work that leads people to right worship. I want the sign more than I want the destination. I want bigger signs. I want more notable signs. I want my signs to sparkle like Vegas neon to set me and my church apart from the desert around us.*

*You want normal faith in Your name. You want us to live out the restored life. You want this to be our new expectation where Your refreshing comes on us in a chaotic world. You do not want extraordinary or loud; You want a new normal.*

*Help us to walk as children of the prophets and covenant where our lives bless all people groups of the earth. Instead of wanting the signposts, we want the destination of full restoration. Thank You for providing the refreshing waves of Your presence as we travel this path.*

*I pray we have healing in the house of prayer so we have healing to offer the world. I pray we have the new normal of praise to offer on the other side of the signs. I pray we do not become discouraged with the rugged terrain—the terrain merely speaks to the need for the final destination.*

*Thank You! I praise Your name as I pray, "Thy kingdom come, Thy will be done."*

*Amen*

Thank you for walking with me through Acts 3. Perhaps the passage calls you to look in the direction of the destination rather than being satisfied with momentary signs. If your experience is like mine, then you too get discouraged with the reduction of signs when we focus on them rather than the place where all things find restoration. Be refreshed. Acknowledge your empty pockets. Express faith in His name. Who knows—you may pass a person in need today. What do you have to offer?

God bless,

Jim

# 28 | A *WALK* THROUGH ACTS 4

According to Statista.com, advertising expenditures in the US totaled about $195.8 billion in 2016. When compared to data from Giving USA, advertising companies receive about seventy-five billion more dollars per year than do religious institutions. Evidently people believe advertising works. Some advertising happens on a large scale and is addressed to everyone. Micro-advertising also happens when web pages use information from my searches to tailor make ads aimed at me.

In my naiveté, I thought this was an interesting coincidence the first time I saw an ad for my favorite pair of shoes as I read through a news blog. When an ad for my wood carving chisels came up next, I realized my search engine, news blog, product vendors, and marketing firms contributed to this conspiracy. Privacy does not exist anymore. I wonder when we'll see Hollywood's idea that facial recognition software will combine with marketing to create digital billboards that match my own purchasing preferences. Stores already track my purchases through customer loyalty cards where they get me to voluntarily give them my information to help them tailor advertising just for me.

I do not generally give way to conspiracy theories. I think Elvis is dead. The astronauts did land on the moon. I tend to believe Lee Harvey Oswald shot JFK. I do not think President

Bush conspired to bring down the Twin Towers. But I do think advertising is a conspiracy to get what few dollars I have and to entice me to mortgage the ones I may get in the future.

As I walk through Acts 4, I cannot help but see the conspiracy of the fallen world against God's purposes and care. I find the single-minded focus of God and His people to be even more amazing. Fortunately faith tells us which side will win! This faith does not rest in some future promise in Heaven; rather, it rests in the death, burial, and resurrection of Jesus. This tells us why Peter preached the same Crucifixion and Resurrection message in his first three recorded sermons.

Peter drew from David's words in Psalm 2 where all the heathen joined together against Christ before he enumerated the diverse groups that conspired to bring about Jesus' death. Yet they only achieved what God had already determined to do! God even uses fallen powers to bring about His number one initiative—the restitution of all things (Acts 3:21).

The lame man. Two apostles on the way to prayer. The angry priestly clan. The five thousand newly converted men and their families. The unified prayer meeting. All of these elements of Acts 4 participate in one snapshot of God's eternal plan to restore all things to Himself.

I cannot help but compare the early church's response to organized opposition to the response I feel in my own spirit and in the lives of many people around me. Where I see isolated vignettes of suffering and slander, the early church saw God's orchestrated work to restore. The man healed after more than forty years of being lame served as irrefutable evidence that Jesus rose from the dead. Neither the healed man, nor the angry priests, nor the scolded disciples played a central role in the story. The resurrected Christ set the agenda. The story points to Him alone.

Perhaps the disciples' prayer provides a wonderful corrective for my own prayer life and perspective of crises in my life. Their simple prayer had three elements: 1) see what they are doing, 2) grant us boldness to speak the word, and 3) stretch forth Your hand to heal with signs and wonders by Thy holy child Jesus.

They did not pray for freedom.

They did not pray for vengeance.

They did not pray for respect.

They did not pray for restoration of some golden age from the past.

Their prayer assumed that the same hand worked in the present circumstance as had worked in aligning the fallen powers against Jesus. The hand allowed Jesus to die. The hand resurrected Jesus. The hand sent them into the world. The hand healed and would heal again.

Their prayers were answered . . . and more. The Holy Spirit filled them afresh. The place shook. They spoke with boldness. They shared all they had with each other. The apostles witnessed the Resurrection with power. Greater grace came upon all. The conspiracy of fallen powers did not stand a chance against God and His unified people.

I think I want that more than my freedom, vengeance, respect, or a golden age that does not exist.

I think I need to pray.

---

*Dear Jesus,*

*I repent. As Peter said in Acts 3, times of refreshing come when I repent. The Acts 4 story shows me I have more opportunities to repent and to see greater grace. I turn from seeing my own story as the central theme and major concern. I turn toward seeing Your purposes in restoring all things to Yourself. Your eternal purpose must have top billing in my prayers, affections, and actions. I want to find my deepest joy in living out my small part in Your universe-sized restoration plan.*

*Lord, You see what is ordered against Your people today. Rather than respect, I want boldness to love the lame and the broken—boldness to see healing of the world's hurts as evidence of Your resurrection and reason to be hauled into public scrutiny and boldness to pray for and care for others more than I pray for myself. Please, Lord, use Your hand to bring signs and wonders by Your apostles and prophets today. Then give us the boldness to use those signs to point to Your resurrection—the hope for all humanity.*

*I pray this with my brothers and sisters. We want to properly understand angry words against us as the death rattle of the fallen powers. We anticipate fresh evidence of Your Spirit. We look forward to a shaking that must happen in us before the world can be shaken. We look forward to sharing our resources with each other as You prepare to share us with the world.*

*Please, Lord, "Do whatsoever thy hand and thy counsel determined before to be done" as Your kingdom comes and Your will is done on earth (Acts 4:28).*

*In Jesus' name,*

*Amen.*

---

Thank you for walking with me through Acts 4 today. Perhaps you too stand in awe of both God's determination to restore all things to Himself and His decision to use us in that process. I invite you to reorder your thoughts and prayers with me as we look for fresh signs and wonders to be done. Did you just feel the earth move under your feet?

God bless,

Jim

# 29 | A *WALK* THROUGH ACTS 5

As a child I participated in an ancient art form. Someone bought me a little red metal loom with multi-colored stretch loops. My not-so-nimble fingers used the coat hanger-like hook to make potholders. Mom still had some of those prized possessions long after I grew into adulthood. Somehow I do not think those pieces of functional kitchen "art" will measure up to the value of the seventeenth-century Persian Vase Rug that recently sold at Sotheby's for just under $34 million. The rug represents the height of the art form developed in the Kerman region of Persia—an isolated providence that could develop the art because it escaped the devastating series of invasions experienced by neighboring regions.

Archeologists have found evidence of weaving in every major civilization in the world. Before humans could write, they could weave. While materials and technology varied, people took thin fibers and wove them into something larger, stronger, and more beautiful. The Bible includes many references to weaving from Joseph's many-colored robe and the Mosaic law's mandates on purity of woven material to Lydia's dyeing business and Tabitha's garment-making compassion ministry.

The invention of the cotton gin and mechanized looms took weaving out of cottages and into factories. Weaving helped fuel the industrial revolution that radically transformed human culture. More recent globalization of technology and commerce has emptied most of the mill towns of the Western world in the search for cheaper labor in Asia. Yet native crafts-people from around the world and young children with their little looms still practice this connection to our ancestors.

Perhaps weaving represents our interconnectedness better than any other human experience. Pulling one thread or changing a series of patterns impacts the whole piece. Walking through Acts 5 illustrates both the wonders and threats to the unity of God's mission in the world. As Peter and the apostles mentioned, all they had to do was witness what they had seen. Witnessing required remaining faithful to each other and to the leading of the Spirit.

Strangely the only real threat to the Master's weaving mission came from the inside. A couple of saints wanted to act like they fully participated in the mission, as did Barnabas from the previous chapter, but they retained some of the property's purchase price for themselves. Rather than remaining true to the Weaver, they had let Satan fill their hearts. The language of the text seems to convey an effort to falsify the Spirit in their lives. They wanted to act like they followed the Spirit rather than doing so. Such counterfeiting betrayed both the community of believers and the Spirit.

Death came. And then death came again.

Strangely, unity followed.

Signs and wonders flourished at the hands of the apostles as they wove their way through the public spaces around the Temple. Male and female believers allowed the Weaver to insert their lives into the tapestry. Hope abounded for the sick and demon-tormented people who could get within a shadow's reach of the apostles.

From my contemporary location, I would think imprisonment, ordering of the establishment against the church, and beatings would have threatened the church's unity and mission faithfulness. Such actions had disrupted the messianic claims of previous contenders as narrated by Gamaliel, but this time the followers joined together instead of slinking their way back to anonymity. The lashes brought whelps of rejoicing rather than angry screams for revenge or whimpers for relief. They rejoiced over the privilege to be "counted worthy to suffer shame for his name" (Acts 5:41).

What appears to be mistakes or flaws in our tapestry may in fact be our greatest strength. Just as prize burl wood develops because of an injury, virus, or fungus, those things that we expect to bring tears result in beauty. What we think harms our chances to fulfill God's purposes draws us nearer to the One who entered our world and changed the pattern of our lives to fulfill His plan. Beatings sent the early church back to the Temple and to fellowship from house to house where they "ceased not to teach and preach Jesus Christ" (Acts 5:42).

Here I thought my difficult year posed a threat. Perhaps the Weaver has been at work once again.

I think it is time to pray.

*Dear Jesus,*

*Forgive me, I pray. At times I try to shield part of myself from Your body to protect myself from what threatens the natural man. Such actions come dangerously close to falsifying the Spirit as did Ananias and his wife. I sometimes pull back from my brothers and sisters in a way the betrays the fellowship with Your Spirit.*

*Only by Your grace are we sustained as Your people.*

*Not only am I grateful for Your forgiveness, but I am also overjoyed with the new potentials that this season of life provides. What I think blocks the way for Your purposes actually opens a new door to identify even more deeply with Your plan. Renew my mind, spirit, emotions, and actions, I pray, so that I may live my days as reasonable service. Strengthen my witness in public space as well as in fellowship with my brothers and sisters. Failure in either place would represent a step away from Your tapestry design.*

*"Thy kingdom come, Thy will be done in earth."*
*In Jesus' name,*
*Amen*

---

Thank you for walking with me through Acts 5. Perhaps some of the reds in your part of the rug look a little brighter and take on a new meaning more vividly than they did before. Perhaps you too yearn to trust the Master Weaver in a greater dimension as you consider your current situation. Please join with me in celebrating our identity in Christ and anticipating the signs and wonders He will perform through His body during this season. A hurting world awaits the next shuttle move the Weaver has in store for us. If we take over the weaving, maybe we could make a decent potholder out of our lives. If we let Him control the loom, He will complete the treasure without price—the work He has already begun. The sick and demon-possessed await our decision.

God bless,

Jim

# 30 | A *WALK* THROUGH ACTS 6

I hated gym class when I was in school. While I enjoyed playing outdoor sports with my friends and brothers, gym classes filled my heart with dread. In high school I think the credit inequity proved to be a part of the problem; gym class awarded you one quarter credit each year while an academic class gave a full credit. I made sure I had as few gym classes and study halls as possible. Why waste precious learning opportunities with play and homework time? (Home provided the time for that!)

I think part of my dislike for gym class goes back to grade school. Taking academic classes instead of gym at least gave me a decent vocabulary, but even though I was generally taller than my classmates, I had a severe kinesthetic intelligence deficit. My body did not move very well. Paul must have seen people run like me when he said we should not run like one who beats at the air. When cool athletic types got to pick their teams, us air-beaters knew we would be standing on that red line until the very end. Captains would prefer an empty space on the ball field or volleyball court rather than encounter my elbows and knees on a critical play.

So much of life appears to classify humanity into two groups: the haves and the have-nots. The ability to move one's body provides only one example. Finances, musical ability, artistic eye, facility with words, divergent thinking, creativity, political awareness, and so many other areas of life separate people into those two groups. What many of us knew as the IQ test represents an unfortunate example. The test does not measure the practical intelligence needed in farming or plumbing any more than it discerns the ability to recognize musical chords and meter. Fortunately, the IQ test carries far less weight today than it did years ago. Too many people's wisdom got overlooked or demeaned in the intelligence-measuring process.

The church should be one place where the haves and have nots division gets exposed and destroyed. Acts 6 provides three examples of this act of godliness. While we do not know how much time elapsed between Acts 2 and Acts 6, we do see some established behavior patterns emerging. Abiding in apostolic doctrine, fellowship, breaking of bread, prayers, wondrous signs, and shared possessions continued to be the norm. Unfortunately divisions in the surrounding world found mirror examples in the church. Greek-speaking and Greek-cultured Jewish Christian widows did not get the same level of care as the Hebrew-cultured widows. Fortunately the Greek-speaking community murmured against this sin. Fortunately the apostolic leaders recognized the righteousness of their grievance rather than holding on to the young church's tradition. (Yes, every church quickly develops traditions.) As a result, the church developed a proactive way to address the false worthy-of-care and not-worthy-of-care distinction.

The source of authority represents the second example of barrier deconstruction. The apostles refused to hoard power. The leaders called the church together to set the course at this critical juncture. The apostles would not directly provide the oversight of the expanding care ministry, but they would set some useful criteria for the process to follow. To control authority—something they would have seen regularly at the

Temple and government houses—would weaken their ability to fulfill their own leadership roles. The "multitude of disciples" screened the candidates based on the apostles' proposed guidelines. They selected seven worthy candidates. The apostles ordained the seven candidates for this new ministry. The seven deacons received the first church appointment after Pentecost.

The chapter demonstrates the wondrous work of the Holy Spirit. Pentecost said divisions of age, gender, and socio-economic class would finally disappear as controlling categories for the Spirit's work. While we do not know about age, we do know that class differences were obliterated in both those being served and those doing the serving. The Holy Spirit could be seen in wisdom, faith, wonders, and miracles throughout the chapter. The apostle group did not control the Spirit's work. Now non-apostles began to exercise their spiritual gifts. Wonder followed! Church multiplication resulted! Abusive priests (referenced in Acts 5) began to obey the faith!

Overturning ungodly divisions within the body quickly moved into the church's work in the world. Stephen's spiritual wisdom and insight led him to the Greek-speaking synagogues. Evidently this part of the Jewish community had experienced few witnesses in the past, even though they were present in the Acts 2 crowd. Now that divisions faded in the body, the division of worthy and unworthy mission fields crumbled. They would hear. They could not resist Stephen's wisdom and faith. Naturally anger arose because the gospel always mandates "changing the customs," which in this case had stood for so long (Acts 6:14). The bread distributing demonstrates the indivisible relationship between care ministries and what we typically call evangelism outreach. In some ways the deacons took the point of the spear in fulfilling Acts 1:8 in this season of the church's life.

Maybe I need even more "changing the customs" moments than I have had in the past.

I think I need to pray.

---

*Dear Jesus,*

*I need to both repent and rejoice. I really do not know which one to do first, but the joy is bubbling a little too strongly to be suppressed for later in the prayer. Thank You! You never make me or others stay on that red line of shame where we will be picked last. Thank You for including division busting in the outpouring of the Spirit. You force me to release the built-up reservoirs of shame that came from feeling worth less than the cool, star play-ers. You fill all of us, Your people, with the authority and power to do that which You send us to do. If I had the kinesthetic intelligence to do so, I think I would dance right now.*

*I repent of seeing myself and others as unworthy of care, spiritual wisdom, and strength. I repent of seeing some groups of people as problems for the gospel rather than opportunities for the Spirit to do a new work in new places. As I repent, I need the Spirit's work. Where can I spread the bread? How can I listen to the margins of the church and the world without hearing it as criticism? How can I better know my own place of spiritual authority so that I can better enable others to live out their spiritual gifting?*

*Finally, I intercede on behalf of others. Dear Lord, bless my brothers and sisters who occupy the red line of the Last Picked People (LPP). Help them to hear Your words that say the LPP will be first and the first will be the LPP. Help them to feel Your Spirit empower them afresh to live according to Your purposes. Help the LPP value their ability to see the Never Picked People (NPP). Oh Lord! So many NPPs live in cities, countryside, prisons, universities, bridge shadows, subways, Wall Steet, and Hollywood. Oh Lord! Do You still have Stephens and Phillips who see NPPs and speak with authority and compassion? Our world needs them so! The world needs a multiplication of disciples and so many kinds of priests to become obedient to the faith.*

*"Thy kingdom come, Thy will be done."*
*In Jesus' name,*
*Amen*

---

Thank you for walking with me through Acts 6. Perhaps the Spirit nudged you off the LPP red line or opened your eyes to someone on that line. If you have served as an Acts 6 deacon and no one values your work, please know Jesus finds great joy in you. Accept the diaconate (servant) as a leadership role for this last-day revival. We need the apostles. We also need people who can handle bread.

God bless . . . I really mean it. Be blessed,
Jim

# 31 | A *WALK* THROUGH ACTS 7

D ionne Warwick started singing solos and choir numbers in the 1950s. She even organized her own group, The Gospelaires, with her sister and her aunt, Cissy Houston, while still in high school. By the early sixties, her pop music took her to the charts in the US, UK, and Australia. Her recordings turned away from gospel music for nearly forty years until her 2008 album titled *Why We Sing*. Perhaps when she sang "Promises, Promises" in 1968, Warwick revealed some of the challenges and disappointments life's broken promises brought her way. She sang, "My kind of promises can lead to joy and hope and love, yes, love!"

I find myself all mixed up in promises from time to time. My various cultural interactions give different kinds of promises. For example, the university gave me different promises than the media and politics. The economy makes promises. Family and friends make promises. Books make all kinds of promises. The church makes promises. God and the Bible make promises. Of course saying, "I hear God's promises to be . . ." might be more accurate than saying, "God promised this . . ." Like Ms. Warwick, I too want the kind of promises that deliver "joy and hope and love, yes, love!" I think I hear an echo of a preacher's sermon from I Corinthians 13:13 in the refrain.

Faith somehow gets misplaced in the promise jumble. Ms. Warwick was right; such promise jumbles bring destruction and despair.

The record of Stephen's sermon and the sermon's consequences in Acts 7 takes me through a long, meandering journey of promises. The journey goes through both the Old Testament and the Gospels. God promised Abram land and family. Then He gave the patriarch "none inheritance in it, no, not so much as to set his foot" (Acts 7:5). He gave more promises even without land and without a son. God also promised that the family to come would be mistreated pilgrims for four hundred years.

Promises, promises . . .

Stephen artistically tells the story through the patriarchs: Moses, Joshua, David, and Solomon. Sometimes God delayed the promises. Sometimes the Egyptians seemed to eclipse the promises. Sometimes Israel turned from the promises.

I am sure the crowd clapped their hands, swayed to the orator's cadence, and uttered an occasional "amen" as they considered their collective history. Then the preacher became a prophet. The ancestors persecuted the prophets. The current generation joined in the bloodletting. Our behavior can handle finding fault with the past as we arrogantly state how the current generation would have done things differently if we were around back then.

Mob rule took over the collective consciousness as they "gnashed on him with their teeth" and began to stone him (Acts 7:54). The crowd fulfilled the deacon-preacher-prophet's words. The prophet died for speaking what he saw, for explaining why the people had received the fruit of "Oh, promises, promise, my kind of promises."

I do not know if prophets have a much easier path in today's world. For some reason, we draw back from being told what we cannot see. Perhaps our individualistic society makes this challenge even more significant. If God wants to speak, then surely He will speak directly to me rather than through a prophet like He did in the Old and New Testaments. Surely the twenty-first century is not like the first generation of the church. Surely we always see, hear, and obey without the prophet's voice.

Promises, promises. . . my kind of promises. . .

We still do not like prophets in our hometown. We would rather get on a plane (or YouTube) and see what a prophet has to say someplace else. Prophets sometimes seem like a carnival act. We stare at them with fascination and pray they do not speak to us. When they do, we show our teeth rather than our tears.

I think we still have prophet-martyrs today. I know some personally. We cannot get away with stoning them, so we find an excuse to send them away. Life can be much simpler without prophets irritating us with ways we need to live more faithfully. Why must these prophets speak so when we have not received our full inheritance or while we experience our Egyptian abuse?

I wish I could finish reading Acts 7 and say, "See how they hated the prophet then? I know I would be different. After all, I want to hear God's voice." I can't. I've lived in my "promises, promises" too many times. And I have seen too many prophets walk away with broken bones and gaping wounds.

Does it have to be this way?

I think I need to pray.

---

*Dear Jesus,*

*Oh, Lord! My sins nailed You to the cross! And most of those sins came since I received the Holy Spirit nearly fifty years ago. Forgive me for rejecting Your prophetic words when You deliver them in the Word, in Your still small voice, or from the raspy voice of a prophet. Forgive me for making the prophet so hesitant to speak. Forgive us for the wounds we contribute to the roadmap of scars the prophets already carry on their bodies, their minds, their spirits, and their families. Have mercy. Have mercy . . . on us and the prophets.*

*We stone prophets for being right, and we stone them for being wrong. Forgive us, Lord! I do want Your promises rather than my understanding of those promises. I do want ears that hear You through whatever voice You choose to use.*

*I repent of times I have stifled the occasional prophetic word in my own throat. I did not want any more teeth marks on me either. I must confess that I am afraid to speak for You. What if I am wrong? I'll be rejected, and rightly so. What if I am right? Well, I still might be rejected.*

*Please, Lord, trust us with some more prophets! We need them in this day. How else will we know to turn from our own promises to those higher promises—those more demanding and more comforting promises—that come from You?*

*Finally, Lord, please bind up the wounds of our prophets. Heal J--, Oh, Lord, heal J-- I pray. He only wanted to speak for You! I know he is often awkward around others—how could he not be with the eyes and heart You gave him? Comfort his spirit today even as You open his eyes and ears yet again. I pray You never close his eyes even when he asks for it. I pray we never close his mouth. Do the same, I pray, for Your other faithful prophets. We need them.*

*"Thy kingdom come, Thy will be done," . . . even when You speak it through the prophets.*

*In Jesus' name I pray,*
*Amen*

---

Thank you for taking the off-road hike (sorry, not a walk) through Acts 7. If you got this far, then you probably have a few bruises from the climb. I appreciate your company. I do not think I can learn to hear from prophets by myself. I pray you long for their voices as much as I do. Our world needs us to hear the prophets' voices.

God bless,

Jim

# 32 | A *WALK* THROUGH ACTS 8

Back in the 1930s or so, Jean Piaget, a Swiss child psychologist, began to help people understand that learning does not follow a straight path. People do not learn by just adding new blocks of information to the stack like a child attempting to build the highest tower. Instead Piaget proposed that we develop structures of knowledge where we fit new information into our ways of understanding. The structure works until new information does not fit in our old understanding; then the old understandings must go away.

A child, for example, may have a cuddly friend at home called a dog. While getting strolled around the neighborhood, he learns that other four-legged creatures with tails and long noses are dogs. Then he finds a creature that does not have much of a nose at all. Mom confirms his suspicion that this thing might be a dog as well. Now the understanding of dog includes long and nearly absent noses. How wonderful it is to learn about the world! So many things to label dog. Some he can bend over and pet, while others can stand on their hind legs and lick Dad's face. Yet they all fit within the structure of dog.

A trip to Grandma's house shatters the system of knowledge. When he sees a calf in the field, he joyfully calls it a dog. The animal fits all the criteria: four legs, tail, nose, kind of big. Mom uses the laugh that he knows means he just said something funny, so he says it again, "Big dog!" Mom informs him it is a cow. Only some four-legged animals with tails and noses can be called dog; others must be cows. He would later learn goats cannot be called dog or cow.

Our lives as disciples undergo so much learning too! Becoming new creatures includes getting rid of old ways of thinking and being as all things become new. Sometimes the new things fit in old categories, but at other times the new experiences literally blow our minds. I continually wonder at the call to have the mind of Christ. Paul called the church to "let this mind be in you" (Philippians 2:5). The church needed to surrender to this new-mindedness. The process was not complete. Perhaps we can have the mind of Christ. Perhaps we can be holy as God is holy. Perhaps we can even celebrate the call into that way of thinking and being. We mature while never becoming complete until the day we see Him and become like Him.

Acts 8 provides a case study of this change in thinking. Deacon Phillip transitioned to an evangelist as he moved from Jerusalem to Samaria. The city rejoiced as light shattered the darkness. Old categories of shame, control, fear, and manipulation based on sorcery gave way to new Kingdom possibilities. They believed; Phillip baptized them.

Even the ex-sorcerer believed. The one who once controlled the thoughts and behaviors of the city truly believed this new message of Jesus. Baptism put down old behaviors and allegiances. Rather than seeking followers, he became a follower. He observed the mighty works of God done through the deacon-evangelist.

Peter and John laid hands on the baptized gathering. They received the Holy Ghost. Since Simon the sorcerer was not excluded from the narrative, I believe the text leads us to believe he too continued from believing and baptism on to new life in the Spirit.

Now the story takes a twist. Simon, the new convert, offered money to do what Peter did. He too wanted the authority and power to help people receive the Holy Ghost. In his experience, one gained new authority through purchasing it or earned it through suffering at the hands of others.

Simon Peter (from now on Simon I) told Simon the new convert (from now on Simon II) to put away his money for it would perish with him. God's gifts cannot be purchased. Simon II would have no part in the Holy Spirit's work for his heart was not right. Simon II needed to repent. Again.

Simon I discerned the forces at work in Simon II's response. Simon II had bad heart thoughts. He was "in the gall of bitterness, and in the bond of iniquity" (Acts 8:23).

Simon II asked for prayer. The narrator ends the story at this point rather than giving a glimpse of Simon I's hands on Simon II.

Simon I had the right resumé for this encounter. He had experienced the perplexity of great new categories of knowledge ("Thou art the Christ" [Matthew 16:16]) and heard discouraging words of rebuke ("Get thee behind me, Satan" [Matthew 16:23]). New understanding would have to be reconstructed to take in additional information. Simon I had learned the need for prayer to uproot things in his heart. Jesus exposed the weaknesses of Simon's faith even when the apostolic spokesperson professed a commitment to imprisonment and death. Jesus knew Simon I would fail. He also knew the fallen could be restored.

I see myself in Simon II. I marvel at new spiritual insights and experience the thrill of walking in these new potentials. Darkness flees with such new light. Then I see the needs of others and look for ways to bring the light and hope they need. Sometimes I look in the wrong places for the resources to care for others. Sometimes I look for another seminar or another technique to bring the Kingdom to this new dimension.

May the focus on techniques perish with me.

I must repent. I must find someone to pray for me. I need to discover a faith flaw (Simon I) or bitterness from the past that still flavors our walk with God (Simon II). I need to receive correction from our spiritual leaders (Simons I and II). I must realize these new ways of thinking will continue to claim me, to disorient my old way of thinking and behaving.

I think I need to pray!

---

*Dear Jesus,*

*First of all, thank You for all of the past learning! The years have presented many new opportunities to exchange personal, limited understandings for knowledge more in line with Your eternal principles.*

*Thank You for the gift of correction. Remaining open to new possibilities also provides new opportunities to reject pride. Humility invites us to follow the Spirit.*

*Today fellowship with a dear ministry couple exposed some of those roots like Simon I and II experienced. I had to confess a spiritual weakness that keeps me from completing a ministry task. Too often I fear rejection or living a life of little value. My understanding moves slowly in the direction You call me to go. Faithfulness in this task should be the reward. Like Simon II, I cannot earn the gift of blessing others. Like Simon I, my faith needs strengthening.*

*Thank you for the wonder of praying brothers and sisters! Confession and prayer in Your family brings such healing as James described in the conclusion of his book. I stand in need of this prayer as did Simon I and II—such prayer carries the power of Elijah.*

*Teach us to let go of weaker understandings as You show us the resources needed to bring Your gifts to a hurting world. We cannot do it with our old, limited knowledge.*

"*Thy kingdom come, Thy will be done!*"
*In Jesus' name,*
*Amen*

---

Thank you for walking with me through Acts 8. Maybe the walk reminded you of significant periods where your understanding changed. I pray the crisis of faith, ministry, health, rebuke from a loving brother or sister, or suffering has helped you mature and follow the Spirit's invitation to participate in His work in the world.

God bless,
Jim

# 33 | A *WALK* THROUGH ACTS 9

Perhaps most of us have had them. They started with such creative anticipation that we could not wait to get started. We see the underappreciated specimen that simply begs to be lovingly cajoled back into a state of notability, reclaimed from the refuse pile to serve as an exemplar once again of what "it" was originally designed to be. In some instances, we even dream of improvising on the original product with modern stylistic or technological improvements.

The term *basket case* might be appropriate for an item we can't bear to part with, but perhaps others would think belonged in a wastebasket. I am sure such basket cases have been around for thousands of years. We finally get the motorcycle, truck, house, clock, rocking chair, or quilt at a price that makes restoration possible. We dismantle the various pieces with care. Each step gets archived with cell phone snapshots as we discover the inner workings of the object. If videoing the process, then we would also capture the occasional groan as we uncover unanticipated wear, or gleeful shouts of joy that escape when we find the delightful inner workings left behind by a long-forgotten craftsman. Fortunately cell phones have not evolved to the place where they also capture the musty smells of tired yesterdays.

Acts 9 powerfully records varying layers of God's basket case project of restoring all of creation. In fact, this basket case occupies all of His power and authority. He so loved the basket case that He gave His only begotten Son. The resurrected Son revealed His strategic choice to commission, empower, and send His followers into the basket-restoration work of making disciples.

I stand in awe at God's ability to use unlikely situations for His reconstruction project. Zealots who thought they had God figured out can hear from God, be blinded to stop their running, and receive a godly commission through the hands of a normal disciple. The zealot Saul had not received a word about merely going to Heaven. God had a much larger plan than that. Nations, kings, and his kinsmen would hear of God's grace through Saul. Suffering would be a normal part of the process rather than something to be avoided in a prayer meeting.

Normal disciples would learn to answer, "Here am I," as did the lad Samuel many centuries before. Normal disciples would experience and express their fear when God chose to expand His body to do His work. Expansion always presents new anxieties. The Remodeler, however, is always present in His Spirit to replace fear with open hospitality. Such work far exceeds a mere "salvation experience." Being saved changed the zealots and mobilized the fearful.

The gospel spread.

After the wicker elevator got Saul out of one trap, he found himself facing another issue: doubters in the church. Barnabas served as Ananias had in previous days of tension. Testimony became the key resource for pulling the believers together. Barnabas and Saul told the story. Anxieties reduced within the body so they could face the doubts outside of the body. The gospel spread. New threats came. Basket-case Saul still had revelations to receive and maturity to experience. Many miles lay in front of him. He would die, but not that day.

The fear-filled church experienced some maturation. This one church spread from Judea and Galilee and on to Samaria. Peace and growth came as they feared the Lord, learned to be comforted by the Holy Spirit, and incorporated new believers—all normal stuff for the Basket Case Remodeler!

Acts 9 does not end with this preface to world evangelism. More remodeling needed to be done. The church needed to see some paralytics raised, deceased caregivers valued, and dead brought back to life. The Basket Case Remodeler could be seen in the minds, hands, and hearts of His people.

His plan for reclamation of the world remains the same today.

I think I need to pray.

---

*Dear Lord,*

*Remodeling always requires deconstruction, purifying, and reassembling with purpose. I celebrate all the wonderful evidence of Your basket case work that I have seen over my lifetime. You have blessed my path with evidence of Your reclamation work that parallels Acts 9.*

*When I read of the violence and fear in this single chapter, I realize so little has changed in the process. Do You ever grow weary of confronting Your church as You call us to live out Your mission? Do You grow weary of resistance when You bring in ex-zealots to do worldwide transformation? Could You heal our eyes and ears so we can receive those who once hated us rather than hide in fear and self-defensiveness? How many Sauls sit in blind confusion, waiting for normal disciples to bring a commission rather than "just" the opportunity to be saved?*

*Help me to say "Here I am" to Your call and commission today as I pray for Your kingdom to be on earth as it is in Heaven.*
*In Jesus' name,*
*Amen*

---

Thank you for walking with me through Acts 9. I know the Remodeler has done many restoration acts in your life. Join with me in anticipating newly remodeled believers. Let's welcome them, introducing the Remodeler to other believers, and confirming the Holy Spirit's word that He has much work for them to do in the world.

God bless,
Jim

# 34 | A *WALK* THROUGH ACTS 10

Where does all that antiseptic hand sanitizer come from? When did folks start scrubbing down for surgery after every handshake, using a public computer, or touching a doorknob? I remember the funny stories about Howard Hughes when he passed away in 1976. He would fit right in with many folks in the twenty-first century with his germaphobia. Then he had to live in a hotel penthouse suite; now he could walk around knowing sanitizer would always be within his reach. No one would stare if he chose to wear a mask while taking a walk for his constitution through the germ-coughing masses outside his door.

I appreciate the need for clean hands; I really do. But do I need to lather down every five minutes? Do I always need a bottle within reach? Must I have a dispenser dangling from my briefcase and rearview mirror like someone wearing a garlic garland to ward off vampires? Maybe I am too insensitive to killer germs around me. Maybe we need the half-gallon containers at the end of every church aisle. Just be careful; you do not know who touched the pump last.

I do not know how I survived childhood in a world without hand sanitizer. I also wonder if it is okay to ride on this public airplane right now. Yuck! Maybe I should have hired a hazmat team to scour those bathrooms between Dallas and my destination in Ohio after all.

Reading through Acts 10 transports us to a world even more obsessed with clean and unclean hands. While perceptions of cleanliness differed quite a bit from our day, they nonetheless dominated people's thinking and actions. Every encounter included mandatory considerations of maintaining purity at all costs. Staying clean required constant vigilance of every person one might encounter. Peter put it this way, "You yourselves know how unlawful it is for a Jew to associate with or to visit anyone of another nation" (Acts 10:28, ESV).

While the vision contained a divine mandate to never judge a person to be unclean based on old rubrics, Peter still had no clue why visions and angelic visitations had arranged the meeting. Peter had to ask why Cornelius had invited him to his house.

The soldier explained the angel's appearance—an appearance that included promises that prayers and care for the poor continually stood before God. The heavenly messenger assured the God-fearing soldier that Peter would be able to give divine guidance for him, his family, and close friends that crowded into the house. Cornelius believed the angel and graciously accepted the rare act of a Jew visiting his home. He prophetically claimed, "We are all here in the presence of God" (Acts 10:33, ESV).

Peter witnessed to everything he had seen concerning Jesus from the baptism of John the Baptist to the Resurrection. He told of his own commission to preach Jesus as the Judge and as the One who would grant forgiveness to anyone who asked. He did not preach about the Holy Spirit. The apostle no longer considered them to be unclean, but he did not really see them as potential covenant members.

The Spirit fell on them anyway.

What once required over three years of study and ten days of waiting in an upper room now happened "while Peter was still saying these things" (Acts 10:44, ESV). Jesus not only provided a way to take away uncleanliness, He inhabited all of the Italian outsiders at the same moment. Those of the circumcision were amazed. Peter's friends had come to defend the apostle's purity to people at home; instead they witnessed the birth of brothers and sisters who smelled a little different from them.

In my world I see so much sin stain and differences among people. Oftentimes believers cannot practice fellowship with each other, much less practice hospitality with the "unclean." Maybe we need a vision. Maybe the heavens would open for us when we pray with a hungry stomach. Maybe we could spend some time pondering the vision in the context of cultural exchanges we encounter every day. Just maybe we could invite them into our house. Maybe we could listen until they invited us into their house. Maybe we could hear the angelic proclamation that the prayers of people who do not even know Jesus' name have mixed with their good works to become a holy scent in heavenly places.

Maybe we can witness what we have seen even while we really do not know the dimensions of God's new work. Just maybe the Spirit will fall on whole houses while we talk.

I think I need to pray.

---

*Dear Lord,*

*I worship You, the One who ripped down every cultural barrier by Your death. I worship You, the One who hears prayers, sees when we care for others, and makes us clean where we were once outcasts. As I worship You and give thanks, I must ask for Your forgiveness. I am a man of weak perception and I dwell among a people of weak perceptions. Help us to get along in fellowship and communion in Your body so that we can see Your vision.*

*You have already prepared the way for many Spirit out-pourings—outpourings that will leave us amazed as were the insiders that day. Help us overcome our phobias about a sinful world. You will keep us clean wherever You send us. Your holiness will spread like an unstoppable tsunami.*

*Here I am. I listen for the knock on the door from someone I have trouble believing can be saved so easily. I tend to think more of the evil around me than the good You have placed within me. By Your grace, endow me with the curiosity to visit their houses. I look forward to hearing what You have already told them before I get there. I await Your Spirit's outpouring.*

*Even so, come quickly, Lord Jesus. Let Your kingdom be on earth as it is in Heaven.*

*In Jesus' name,*

*Amen*

---

Thank you for walking with me through Acts 10. I know the Vision Giver and Angel Sender is still at work in our day. I believe we can anticipate the breath of the Holy Spirit reaching into communities we thought were unreachable. Can you feel the anticipation building?

God bless,

Jim

# 35 | A *WALK* THROUGH ACTS 11

Public discourse seems to have lost its civility these days. Periods of rapid social upheaval contribute to a combustible atmosphere where even moderately heated discussions create flash fires and ground-shaking explosions. As a lifelong member of academic communities (from the beginning of my academic career at five years old in Galatia, Illinois, to receiving professor emeritus status from Urshan Graduate School of Theology at age fifty-five), I always thought universities were places to explore ideas in a respectful way. Now major universities have "safe zones" where students can hide from ideas that challenge or threaten them.

Safe zones supposedly protect students from encountering emotionally challenging ideas. Proponents suggest such places always keep students emotionally comfortable. While the image of God should never be attacked in a person by considering them less valuable than the majority group, constant emotional comfort is not an option for adults or even children. The freedom to discuss ideas, respectfully challenge positions of others, and collect data from various perspectives may be too old-fashioned to support in our diverse world.

Shuttering places that share diverse ideas kills the perspective-taking needed to understand others. Refusing to listen hardens differences and actively contributes to culture wars, civil unrest, and conditions for violence.

Not every idea is good. Not every perspective will stand the test of time. But healing cannot happen until voices can be respected enough to be heard. Historically, silencing opposing voices has led to dictatorships that often progress from silencing voices to murder and genocide in the guise of creating a safer, purer environment for a brighter future. If this is true of society in general, how much more it is true for the church?

Luke's story that began with angel voices announcing John the Baptist's and Jesus' birth continued through to the disciples taking the good news to the world. Many growth moments sprang from the soil of misunderstanding and disagreement. I often wonder how the Holy Spirit could work with such people. Then hope breathes again in my chest. Maybe the Holy Spirit can still work with such people like me today.

Reading Acts 11 reveals Luke's appreciation for redundancy. He frequently retells stories to help the reader see beyond the travelogue surface of his gospel. Like a historian from the last generation, Kenneth Scott Latourette, Luke told the story of missionary work rather than a diary of events. Retelling the story reveals the key actors, the plot, and the conflict. Jesus was always the key actor. The plot always led to multiplication of disciples. More conflict came from within the church than from the society around them.

In Acts 11, Luke exposed threats to missional faithfulness by celebrating the Spirit's work in settling disagreements. The Spirit worked to encourage the "conservative" leaders to confront the "liberal" leaders. Conservative forces sought to keep the church the way it was: limited to the Jewish believers. The Spirit helped Peter serve as a transitional leader to hear God's voice by reflecting on the past events, truly hearing the concerns of his brothers, and telling the story of God's grace. The Spirit freed the troubled leaders to be silent as they listened and then glorify God in wonder of the Kingdom's expansion to the Gentiles.

What resulted from the church listening to the Spirit and to each other? "The hand of the Lord was with them, and a great number who believed turned to the Lord" (Acts 11:21, ESV). The Spirit did not stop with resolving the conflict and adding new believers. Jesus' declaration that all power was His and He would use that power to make disciples can be seen in Acts 11. New converts required discipleship. The church sent a good, Spirit-filled man of faith named Barnabas to bring spiritual infants through a season of maturation.

For a whole year, Barnabas and Saul met with the church and taught them. They knew the wonder of new birth. They could celebrate the phenomenon of a transformed life, but they needed instruction in purposefully living out the ways of Jesus. People who never saw Jesus in the flesh became known as Christ followers because of Barnabas and Saul's discipleship ministry. The same power that made the crowd say Peter had been with Jesus (Acts 4:13) now made a new generation of saints from a completely different culture "faithful to the Lord with steadfast purpose" (Acts 11:23, ESV).

These new parts of the church did not carry a stigma of "our generation" or "our culture." They became part of the culture of Christ even though their journey to faith looked different from the established church. Their worship looked a bit different with strange languages and other cultural differences. Yet they knew they belonged to the same faith family. When famine came to the established church, the new believers did the work of a disciple—they provided care for brothers and sisters in need.

Acts 11 was not the first or last occasion of sharp disagreement in the early church. Strong leaders with equally strong opinions on how the church should navigate change had to repeatedly take the risk of sharing their differences, hearing the perspectives of others, and listening for the Spirit to guide them through treacherous confluences. Caring enough for the gospel, each other, and the mission instilled this apostolic method of conflict resolution.

I think I need to pray.

---

*Dear Lord,*

*I repent of moments when I shied away from conflict to just get along. I know I tend to keep the peace rather than see the creative work of the Spirit in times when brothers and sisters lovingly share their understanding of the mission. Have mercy on us, Oh, Lord! Make us a people of Your goodness, Spirit, and faith like Barnabas. Help us to understand Your safe zones always explore differences no matter how painful the process may be. Your safe zones come equipped with grace and spiritual giftings to help us speak and listen respectfully. Help us to leave those rooms as worshiping missionaries ready to transition new converts into disciples that have been with You.*

*"Thy kingdom come, Thy will be done."*

*In Jesus' name,*

*Amen*

---

Thank you for walking with me through Acts 11. I trust the stroll enabled you to remove some of the barriers to hearing brothers and sisters who appear a little different from you. The Spirit is preparing us to welcome many more once "strange" people to the family.

God bless,

Jim Littles

# 36 | A *WALK* THROUGH ACTS 12

E very family has a sleepwalking story or two. Those stories get told at family gatherings where members feel safe; they can celebrate belonging enough to recount the events with laughter rather than shame. My family has old sleepwalking stories from when we were children as well as new ones now that our family has expanded to include in-law daughter and sons. Sorry, I can't tell those stories now, though they bring a smile to my face just thinking about them and anticipating the family get-togethers this fall.

Perhaps you have never experienced sleepwalking, but we all know what it is like to do automatic driving. We have gone down the same road so many times that we no longer see the passing scenery or the pilots of neighboring missiles zipping down the highway at ten miles over the speed limit. As we shut off the ignition at home, we wonder how we got there.

Peter slept. The night awaiting execution in a cell where his good friend James's life had ended with a sword was not enough to keep him awake. Luke carefully points to the calendar as well. The Passover ten or eleven years before had brought him the greatest shame he had ever experienced. Somewhere in that decade Jesus' recall recorded in John 21 had wiped away all shame. Maybe placing his hands on another sinner who thought he had no hope gave him the opportunity to recount his own "unforgivable" past that could not block the power of God's love. He slept shamelessly, freed from worry. The church would survive without him. The Holy Spirit would see to that. He was about to experience the transition from this life to the next. That last journey held joyfully anticipated mysteries. Even prison shackles could not disrupt his sleep.

Acts celebrates many prayer and prison stories. Prayer tuned the saints' lives for Kingdom purposes and opened their eyes to what God planned for them. (Spoiler alert: chapter 13 will start with another prayer meeting.) Prayer revealed open doors. So did prisons. They were free in every location, so incarceration just provided another context for the Holy Spirit to do His work. They expected imprisonment for the gospel. The sharp contrast between the light of the gospel and darkness of sin around them guaranteed jail time. They worked toward overthrowing the darkness rather than overthrowing governments.

Peter did not know he was free until he reached the street. The angel's job, girding up his cloak and lacing his sandals, didn't arouse him. The street did. Once awakened, his first thought was to go to a prayer meeting at a saint's house. The meeting was just a bunch of saints praying in one of the sister's residences. The leaders were not in attendance; the saints followed the Spirit's lead in prayer. Peter wanted to be there to share the testimony of divine deliverance.

Then Peter just left and "went to another place" (Acts 12:17, ESV). We only see the apostle one more time in Acts 15 when he reminds the church of the day the Lord opened the door to the Gentiles. Then he faded away. The lead apostle acknowledged James who took the visible leadership position now. And the church multiplied.

Meanwhile soldiers died for losing their charge. The penalty for the prisoner became their own as was customary for the day. (Hmm, this sounds like Jesus' own death for letting us go free.) Herod would die more slowly than they did. Due to his pride, the Roman vassal received an angelic visitation as did Peter. He died of some intestinal worm disease. Josephus said it took him four or five days to succumb to their infestation. I doubt he slept very much.

Acts 12 ends quietly. Luke simply gave the plans for a four-hundred-mile trip by Barnabas, Saul, and John Mark (the one nourished on prayer in his mother's house). The two evangelists had finished their mission to deliver financial aid to the Jerusalem church, so they went back to their disciples in Antioch. While Peter would only get one more mention in Acts, the Spirit was about to do an amazing new thing through these three men even though they did not know it at the time.

Peter didn't mind. His sleepiness was not the lethargy he exhibited when he slept through Jesus' prayer meeting; it was contentment that his whole life belonged to the Lord. The Lord could use him in accordance with His purposes. To live or die was the Lord's good pleasure. The Lord's plan would be achieved in startling and unexpected ways, and the Lord alone would be glorified. No wonder he slept. Psalm 127:2 had never been truer.

I think I need to pray.

---

*Dear Jesus,*

*Sometimes I sleepwalk and sometimes I just can't sleep. I sleepwalk when my life has become automated with little appreciation for the work You want to do today and little anticipation for what is to come. Have mercy. How many angels have I missed?*

*You are calling me to a peaceful existence in a turbulent world, a place where I can find rest in prison or in the prayer meeting. I must trust Your divine leadership plans and step aside to whatever work You have next for me.*

*I wonder what awaits the church in these troubling times. I know You have something mighty in store for the church on behalf of the world. I look forward to laboring with others in whatever small or big place You have for us. You will get all the glory.*

*We will find our rest in You without fear of sword, gut worms, or of being without value in Your body. You have promised to lead us. We will follow.*

*"Thy kingdom come, Thy will be done."*

*In Jesus' name,*

*Amen*

---

Thank you for walking with me through Acts 12. The Spirit will equip us as He did those early disciples so that we find our deepest rest in His presence regardless of the storms that circle around us. He is faithful!

God bless,

Jim

# 37 | A *WALK* THROUGH ACTS 13

Living in Missouri for twenty-one years provided the opportunity to go to Branson, a cultural center for some Midwest
folks, on quite a few occasions. The trip always included visiting at least one of the entertainment palaces: country music,
comedians, troubadours on horseback to accompany meals
eaten with fingers, outdoor dramas, biblical character productions, Asian jugglers, and magicians. I tend to enjoy most
productions because of the fellowship with friends and family sitting with me. One venue, however, had to be endured
through sheer will power. For me, attending magic shows rates
right down there with root canals and colonoscopies.

Other audience members audibly respond to the tricks
while I selfishly wish someone would pull the fire alarm to put
me out of my misery. For some reason the tricks do not pique
my curiosity. I can't make myself care enough to figure out
how the hankies change color or how the lovely assistant gets
bloodlessly bifurcated. I know they are highly skilled craftsman; I just find more excitement in watching small ripples in
a quiet pond at a much cheaper price point.

Magic is not so innocuous in some parts of the world.
Witch doctors control villages in many cultures. Powerful
world figures consult them to make important decisions.
That kind of magic goes back beyond the days of King Saul.

In Acts 13 we see an apostolic encounter with a sorcerer or magician. The encounter made visible the protestations of evil ordered against the dawning of a new day in God's salvation history. Bar-Jesus, the Jewish magician, saw the threat to his power position. He misrepresented the Lord's straight way and sought to keep the governor from the faith.

Other established Jewish leaders reacted in a similar way to the upstart Jewish sect. They heard the same message as the common Jew and God-fearing Gentile, but envy kept them from really hearing the Word. Rather than magic, they resorted to their position and tradition to stir up the city power brokers.

Acts 13 demonstrates the stark difference between the Holy Spirit on one side and the human defenses of witchcraft and slander on the other. Envy served as a powerful motivator that blocked the ability to see and hear the gracious gospel message. Bar-Jesus was physically blinded for a season while the synagogue leaders experienced spiritual deafness. Paul certainly knew what both gospel responses looked like. At one time he defended what he knew against the new Jewish sect. He too had experienced temporary blindness for his efforts. Paul's solitude prepared him to hear the disciple who would pray and share grace with him. Paul knew how to confront the resisters because he once used the same emotional rejections to the preached word.

Have I mentioned that I don't enjoy magic acts?

I really don't like them when I discover my own use of God's gifts devolving into the realm of magic. Sometimes I have used His name as a magical enchantment to get my way. If I call on the name the right way while increasing frequency and fervency, then the door should open as I want like Alibaba and the forty thieves chanting, "Open Sesame."

I have seen well-meaning people use church attendance, fasting, holiness, and tithing as magical tokens, as if these talismans would protect us from physical, financial, and spiritual evil. We think to ourselves, "If I do these things, then I should not have to actually *walk* through the valley of shadow of death."

While all these practices have tremendous value for followers of Christ, they are not magical tools to get our way. Envy and pride blocked Bar-Jesus and the synagogue leaders from seeing the Holy Spirit work, the Word preached, and grace dispensed.

If I am not careful, I could miss God's missionary work in the world today because a magical gospel protects who I am rather than propels me into the world as salt and light. Paul and Barnabas used the same texts and synagogue structure to proclaim the gospel, but they did so on behalf of the world as witnesses sent by the Spirit.

What results came from authentic use of spiritual resources?

- The Word was preached.
- Jews and Gentiles heard and asked for more.
- People were filled with the Holy Spirit, gladness, and joy.
- A promising mentee withdrew from the team and went home to safer prayer meetings.
- The disciple team got kicked out of town.
- The mission continued to the next city.

I think I need to pray.

---

*Dear Jesus,*
*Thank You for all those prayer meetings with teachers, prophets, and other saints. The Spirit spoke. Thank You for letting me know that even when I pray alone, I pray with my brothers and sisters. The Spirit still speaks!*

*Thank you for sending us into the world today just as you sent Barnabas and Saul in Acts 13.*

*I repent of defensive prayers and attitudes towards those who do not yet see. I repent of taking rejection personally when I have honestly taught the Word to people in need.*

*But I really must intercede for forgiveness for efforts to control the moving of the Spirit through some kind of holy magic. I truly do not want controllable grace or programed witness to the world. I do not want to control others, for then I would rely on my own ability and want the glory for myself. You want to do a different, unbelievable work for all people.*

*As I turn from magical use of Your name and spiritual disciplines, I pray that my spirit opens to the wonder work You are doing in the world today (Acts 13:41). I pray for humility to see all the Spirit's work in the lives of my brothers and sisters. When we follow the Spirit's directions, then the contrast between a dark world and the gospel light will be sharpened. Hungry people will follow. Temporary blindness will lead some to reflect on the Light. Defensive spirits will be exposed.*

*You will be glorified. Your kingdom will come, and Your will shall be done.*

*In Jesus' name,*
*Amen*

---

Thank you for walking with me through Acts 13. I pray my reflections help you consider the power of praying with other leaders. I pray they also help you feel a release to trust the blowing of the Holy Spirit in this new season of your life.

God bless,

Jim

# 38 | A *WALK* THROUGH ACTS 14

Perhaps we have all heard someone exclaim, "That will leave a mark!" after witnessing an accident of some type or seeing a particularly vicious-looking weapon. Both speaker and hearer give thanks for not being a part of the crumpled steel or on the receiving end of the weapon.

Not all marks present themselves for visual inspection. Children who have repeatedly suffered from neglect, violence, or verbal shame carry marks on their spirit. While children are quite resilient in being able to survive harsh circumstances, they carry the marks of abuse where there should be marks of love.

Some external marks do not convey the depth of spirit wounds. Surely the tattoos of holocaust survivors only reveal a tiny amount of the distress they experienced on the inside. Those who suffer violence may have a scar where wounds once oozed the stuff of life, but the trauma of PTSD can shatter spirits for a lifetime. Humans have tools for accurately tracing pock marks on the moon, but we are at a loss to accurately measure marks on the human spirit and the impact of those wounds. Some wounds even get passed from generation to generation. Sin has marked all people, families, and cultures.

As I read Acts 14, I see many mark-leaving events. As I seek to place myself in the traveling disciple band, the sights, sounds, smells, and texture of the marks jump from nearly every sentence Luke transmits to us. I can hear them speak in such a way that a great number of Jews and Greeks believe. The gospel leaves marks that way. The hearer either accepts the grace marks or gives voice to the poisonous marks in their mind. Grace exposes the marks of sin even as it transforms the old wounds into healing paths that draw us to God, each other, and the Master's mission in the world.

When a man who had been unable to walk since birth listened to Paul, he dared to believe twisted limbs could be reformed by grace. When Paul saw faith begin to mark the man's face, he commanded the man to stand. The man's faith went even further; he sprang up and walked. At that moment the whole city saw grace marks and had to respond.

Marks are subject to interpretation. In this case the city misinterpreted the results of grace. Part of their collective psyche was an ancient story of gods visiting their city. The city rejected the gods except for one poor couple. When judgment fell, only the hospitable couple survived. The city went into god-welcoming mode when they saw their brother walk. Unfortunately they did not have adequate experience in reading the signs of grace even though all of nature declared God's grace. Because of grace, God witnessed through the life-giving rains and fruitful seasons that brought gladness even to idol worshipers.

Plans for worshiping Barnabas and Paul as Zeus and Hermes escaped the apostles' attention until the garland-adorned oxen approached the city gates. The priests in their best attire, the glistening knives, and the smiling faces in the crowd told the men what the foreign tongue couldn't: they were about to be worshiped as gods.

They tore their garments to mark the blasphemy of the occasion. Their explanation barely stopped the grievous outcome.

When the two men rejected the crowd's interpretation, the people had to choose between two alternatives. Were these men witness of a new God as they claimed, or were they some malevolent force that came to overturn their city's traditions? Rejecting the praise of humanity frequently leaves a mark. Jesus would not be the kind of king Jerusalem wanted, so honor changed to angry mob action and Jesus' crucifixion. Paul went from a god speaking for Zeus to a villain to be stoned. No middle ground existed. Paul could not accept worship for a while until he could transfer it to Jesus.

They left him for dead. They inadvertently helped Paul clarify his theology.

As the apostles made their way back through the various disciple bands, they encouraged the new believers with a strange message. They would enter the Kingdom by faith and by suffering tribulation. As I sit in on the Bible study held under the flickering light of an oil lamp, the bruises of the speaker must have punctuated the words more than a Hammond B3 organ. The word *tribulation* sounds different when spoken through broken teeth.

The marked man offered his Bible study group the chance to be marked like him. They too would be marked by faith in God's offered grace and marked by the opposition. Evidently enough heard the call as they took the cup and bread that night to call for the appointment of new elders.

As I finish the journey with the missionaries in Acts 14, a journey that required walking sixty to one hundred miles between cities after being left for dead, I must come home to Texas. I cannot stay with them. I cannot worship them any more than the cities could. Like most people I want to leave some kind of mark on the world. But the apostles' words still ring in my ears, and I can still taste the cup and bread—tokens of Jesus' suffering and hope—on my tongue. Am I willing to carry all the marks of grace, or do I want to be worshiped for having done something?

I think this calls me to pray.

---

*Oh Lord,*

*Thank You for your boundless grace! My family and I carry so many grace marks that we have lost count. We know each day starts with new mercies. All we must do is pray and receive.*

*I repent of the various ways I have accepted worship that only belongs to You. Sometimes I have lived faithfully and done good works to be noticed, to find value in that performance. Those efforts marked me and those I served in negative ways. In those moments I have exchanged the boundless love and value You placed on me for my feeble efforts to produce value for myself. Forgive me, I pray! Even now as I pray, I know Your grace washes over me afresh. Today has new grace marks.*

*I pray for the strength we all need to accept and even value the tribulations that accompany entering the Kingdom. Surely identifying with You and Your kingdom will place us in opposition to a world that prefers idols of their own making that they control rather than worshiping the Creator.*

*Finally, I am so blessed that I do not have to walk this way alone. The Holy Spirit guides my brothers, sisters, and me on this Kingdom journey.*

*As I recount my marks today. I give You glory all over again. All glory and honor belong to You. "Thy kingdom come, Thy will be done."*

*In Jesus' name,*
*Amen*

---

Thank you for walking with me through Acts 14. Tracing the steps of faithful men and women in Acts clarifies our own faith journey. Be refreshed in the Spirit as you recognize grace marks in your life. Celebrate God's goodness as you share that grace with others.

God bless,

Jim

# 39 | A *WALK* THROUGH ACTS 15

I miss those days when little people lived in my house. I do not miss the need to buy new sneakers when they outgrew them every three months, and I certainly do not miss parent-teacher conferences, but this morning I am missing the opportunity to share great literature with one of my daughters or my son in my lap after work or before they went to bed. Even before they could understand the words (and thought the pages were for eating rather than enjoying the wonderful illustrations) we would share those moments. I miss reading together the repetitive, rhyming words from *Green Eggs and Ham* by Dr. Seuss evoking all of the places one would *not* want to eat green eggs and ham and the quintessential summary:

I do not like green eggs and ham,

I do not like them Sam-I-am!

Oh, what passion, plot, characterization, and playful use of the language! I have to smile as I think about the building tension in the story as Sam-I-am evangelizes the unnamed Other. Other began by disliking Sam-I-am before disliking his message. Eventually Other overcame his prejudice long enough to sample the delicacy. The story ends with celebration and thanksgiving for Other's stretched palate as well as for Sam-I-am.

Of course, I enjoyed reading Bible stories to my children as well. Oh, what passion, plot, characterization, and playful use of language! How could I not laugh with them as we thought about picking little bugs from our teeth while trying to swallow a camel . . . whether it was one hump or two.

Sometimes the plot got a little too thick to explain to little children. Sometimes the Gordian Knot of disagreements became so entangled that even I had to read and believe without understanding all. While those days with little children in my house are memories from the last millennium, I still wrestle with the plot and promised resolution when all things would be reconciled back to the Creator. I still smile when I read the Word, but I must confess I weep a little too.

Acts 15 could be taken straight from church conferences or ministers' chat pages today. Well-meaning disciples from the Pharisee tradition went from Jerusalem without authorization to make sure the new disciples in Antioch had experienced full salvation. They were appalled to see the lack of circumcision and violation of so many of the 613 laws from the Old Testament. Perhaps they wanted to add many of their own additional protections to the Law to make sure the new Jesus followers kept all the traditions.

Peter listened to the extended debate before responding.

Much debating and much listening play key roles in becoming a missionary people. Passions flare as deep emotions come to light. Each side lines up their arguments like seventeenth-century military tactics that arranged soldiers in nice little rows. Practiced debaters ram the arguments home as so many musket balls driven down the barrel of flintlock weapons. Such rhetoricians live to win, to display the bloodied corpses on the battlefield.

Then someone mentioned God's work, the gospel, the Holy Spirit, faith, and grace. A couple more brothers stood and spoke of signs and wonders in the battlefield—a battlefield of human redemption rather than triumph of one faction over the other.

Then a godly leader placed aside his own preferences to remember prophetic words where both the tent of David and seeking Gentiles would be saved. The mission won. No party lost. The mission won. They wrote a letter and sent it by the hand of two prophets, Barsabbas and Silas. The prophets went into a place filled with "unsettled minds," brought words of encouragement and strength, and left the place occupied by the Prince of Peace.

No party lost. The mission won. Confusion and marginalized status left. Prophets brought healing words.

But wait! As we giggle with hope and healing, the plot thickens once again. Another disagreement comes to the surface between two brothers who had seen the angry mob of disappointed idol worshipers. They could stand together against external threats, but they split over disagreements from within. Jesus promised offenses would come; He even told us the real offenses would come from within the body. Demonic forces could not separate the two apostles. Mobs and government agencies failed to divide them. But considering restoring an immature leader did the trick. A chapter with much hope and grace reminds us that we never will outgrow the need to hear God's voice above the arguments of others. More critically, can we hear God's voice above our own arguments?

God did (and still does) amazing things in sending the gospel to new people groups through His faithful Sam-I-ams of evangelism and care. God still calls Sam-I-ams and Others to focus on the mission rather than the things that separate them.

I prefer to eat green eggs and ham the right way: on a china plate with nice cutlery and a cloth napkin across my lap. I hear that some of my brothers use paper plates and plasticware. I hear some of my sisters scramble their green eggs before mixing them with diced ham and jalapeños in a corn tortilla. Will there be no end to the differences? Can I hear grace speak louder than my preferences as we live the green eggs and ham way in the world? Can I go beyond tolerance of my fellow Southeast Asian culinary experts and assist them as they wrap their green eggs and ham in banana leaves before feeding the hungry? Will we ever stop testing God?

I think I really need to pray.

---

*Lord,*

*Forgive me for avoiding conflicts in the body. I resist the debate to keep the peace. Instead of sharing the responsibility to find missional unity together under the superintending power of the Holy Spirit, I tend to line up the arguments like tin soldiers in my mind. Walls build. I resist the spiritual gifts of others and lose the opportunity to bless others with the grace You have given me.*

*Help me to realize the impact of my inaction—real sufferers in a world that waits for You. Give me the courage to examine the yoke I carry and expect others to carry. Help me to give space for other voices rather than just finding five people who agree with me to settle the point for us.*

*Heal my eyes so I can see again. I really want to see what You are doing in the world today. I really want to see where You call the body to labor together even though our cultural garments, diets, and worship styles may look a little different. Help me to see the vital points of agreement that must be maintained as we labor together. Help me know what does not matter. Help me hear both the strict James-like party and the testimonies of signs and wonders. You have placed so many different people in Your body. Help us labor together for the sake of the mission.*

*Help us make space for immature apprentices when they ask to rejoin the team.*

*Finally, pour more grace on us when we fail to labor together. We must not succumb to cynicism, pride, or despair when we cannot agree. We must learn that offenses will still come from within the body, but Your grace is still sufficient.*

*"Thy kingdom come, Thy will be done."*

*In Jesus' name,*

*Amen*

---

Thank you for walking with me through Acts 15. The journey helps us see that the New Testament gives us both apostolic doctrine and apostolic missional processes. I pray the Lord equips you with a firm foundation and a heart molded by compassion for others. Both key resources can only come from Him. Try a little salsa on your green eggs and ham today!

God bless,

Jim

# 40 | A *WALK* THROUGH ACTS 16

The author of the apostle Paul's biography, *A Man in White,* spent his early adult life in West Germany as a Morse code interceptor for the US Air Force. Sitting at his radio equipment in Europe, he must have felt worlds away from his hometown in impoverished rural Arkansas. The young man excelled at this mission; his officers prescribed amphetamines to keep him alert and on task for longer hours. He would struggle with the resulting drug addiction for much of his life.

Though the young staff sergeant had the best ears and mind in the business, he really wanted to sing. He bought a five-dollar guitar and began to play. He wrote a few songs as well. After watching a movie about prison life in 1951, Sergeant Johnny Cash wrote his song "Folsom Prison Blues" while still in the Air Force. He would record and sing the song several times before performing for the Folsom prisoners in 1968. He said he wrote the startling line "Shot a man in Reno, just to watch him die" after trying to imagine the absolute worst reason for killing another human being. Listening to the recording fifty years later, I was still haunted by the applause from the audience until I learned the producer added the responses in the studio as he prepared the album for release. Folsom Prison sat silent while Mr. Cash yearned for a train to take all of them far from their prison bars. In fact, the man in black felt like all people live behind some prison bars.

Acts 16 recounts prison bars, singing, and true freedom all humanity seeks. The chapter begins with a story to help me realize freedom includes voluntarily laying down my own prerogatives for the good of others. Luke takes his readers from the highly contentious Jerusalem conference, where all agreed not to hold new converts accountable to Jewish traditions, to the circumcision of Timothy under the approving eye of Paul. Fortunately Luke explained the paradox: many Jews were in the mission field and they knew of Timothy's mixed heritage. Timothy lived free from all prison bars—so free that he could give up his own preferences and comforts for the mission. He could volunteer for the painful surgery because of the mission.

Am I that free, or do I hear the gospel train's whistle at a distance? How can I hear the missionary whistle and respond for the needs of others rather than live just for me? How can I love others as Timothy did? Or do I live my life in the condition that German psychologist Eric Fromm calls "escaping from freedom?" Living for self and avoiding the focus needed to live a purposeful existence may look like life without bars, but it actually represents an escaping from freedom to the comfortable confinement of self-imposed prison. Freedom trains can become rolling cells if saints live beneath their missional privilege.

The prison theme becomes even more raw after Paul and Silas bankrupt the local fortune-telling franchise. For some reason the preachers became deeply irritated at the demonic advertisement. They cast out the demon to get a little rest for themselves.

Systems around Jesus' kingdom will always revolt when we witness Kingdom advancement. Those who owned the girl thought this new religion robbed them of their rightful property. Attacking personal property and privacy will bring opposition. I wonder what would happen to the economy if all alcoholics were set free from the bars of their addiction tomorrow? Breweries and taverns would hand out pink slips, and farmers would lose markets. Bottle makers, canning machine manufacturers, and label printers would need to retool. Advertising agencies would have to think of some other use for Clydesdale horses and mountain stream images. The federal government would lose $9.6 billion in excise taxes; ATF would become just TF.

For Paul and Silas, the prison became a space for what they always did—worship. We do not know what was on the police blotter that night, but I wonder what offenses lingered in other cells. The other prisoners listened to the singing that doubtlessly included unintended sour notes and sharp intakes of breath. Rod-ripped flesh and leg shackles restricted movement, but it fueled worship. Worship and prayer during suffering still serves as a primary mission tool. I wonder if I am free enough to be that kind of worshiper.

Walls fell.

Men stayed in their cells. I always thought the supernatural event could be seen in the stone dust in the air and abandoned chains on the ground, but the real power was in all the men staying with the two worshipers. Something rooted them to the ground rather than doing the natural thing after being sprung from prison.

More walls fell for the attempted suicide victim. The warden accepted the reality that his life was forfeited due to the act of God in the earthquake. The worshipers prevented the tragedy by pointing to all the prisoners waiting for instruction. The man used his extra moment of life to ask an important question, "What must I do to be saved?" The question came because free men remained in a prison without bars. Somehow dust-covered wounds convicted the warden of his own sin.

Minions of a police state experienced salvation the same way as everyone else. If he believed in the Lord Jesus, then he and his whole household would be saved. The household undoubtedly included his family as well as servants and employees. Paul shared the gospel in a way that demonstrated the power of being truly free. They all experienced a prison break that night by going down to the river. The warden washed Paul's back while Paul washed the man's and his household's sins away.

Hospitality followed the baptismal service as it did for Lydia's household earlier in the chapter. Hospitality served as a powerful sign of freedom from sin's prison. The chapter ends back at Lydia's house where the believers shared fellowship and heard encouraging words from the bruised men.

I think I need to pray.

---

*Lord,*

*You promised us everlasting life and fathomless joy as part of Your new creation. Forgive me for setting the parameters of that new life through my old eyes. My old eyes see pain-free, luxurious days of ease as freedom. Release from the prison of old eyes lets me know true freedom emancipates me from the restrictions of a self-centered, pleasure-driven existence. You have healed my eyes many times, but I still see a few men as walking trees.*

*Could You help me cast out demons before they irritate me? Would You help me understand the system-shattering effect Your kingdom has on absolutely everything around me? I do not think our world needs another gentle, easily integrated kingdom that looks like just one more software update.*

*Oh! Just to think of the freedom You want to give Your people makes me weep. I do not know the kind of freedom*

*that calls me to stand in the collision between Your king-
dom coming and the entrenched world order. I think my
people and I would rather You just got good people elected
to political office to fix stuff. But You have already walked
us through the choir practices that prepare us for prison
concerts where the stripes may be on our bodies as we sing
of Your goodness to the outcasts. Prison wardens will hear.
Suicide will be prevented. Midnight wound washing and
sin scrubbing will result.*

*Today when I pray, "Thy kingdom come, Thy will be
done," I do believe it sounds differently than it did yesterday. I hear a distant whistle calling me out of my cell;
I think it is the sound of Pentecost.*

*Your grace is sufficient.*

*In Jesus' name,*

*Amen*

---

Thank you for walking with me through Acts 16's prison experience. I pray that prison bars give way for you to live boldly on the mission today. The Master has you right where your life can be a beam of light in a dark world. Live freely, joyfully, and worshipfully in the chaos around you. Perhaps today is the day you get to take someone to the river.

God bless,

Jim

# 41 | A *WALK* THROUGH ACTS 17

I know I am not the only one who thinks he belongs in a different time. I've been a fountain pen user since 1973 when our general conference hotel was next to a drugstore. Like all twelve-year-olds, I had to check out the stationery aisle to see their school supplies. My affair with real writing instruments started with the purchase of a two-dollar Sheaffer fountain pen. This morning I am using a 1950s Conway Stewart No 58 with a wonderful stub-ish medium nib. The sepia ink came from Charles, a good friend in Singapore who gets it. My paper is Japanese Midori paper with heavy cotton content that I pick up when I can stop at Anderson Pens in Appleton, Wisconsin. I know I'll have to use my MacBook later, but I have a few more moments to enjoy the aesthetics of writing the way I like it a bit longer.

I wore bow ties when I had to find vintage ones, have Mom make them, or pay overpriced specialty stores for them. Thankfully they have reached cool status recently, so I am now stocked up for the next fifty years or so. I also wear fedoras rather than baseball caps most of the time.

Some things just cannot be found at a reasonable price. I have yet to find an outlet store with lounging jackets that look like a cross between a tuxedo and a house coat. They are beautiful! People wore them when they read books or dressed for dinner. People did not generally use their car steering wheel as a dining table in those days. Several years ago I found such a robe at an antique store in a beautiful mulberry color. The padded collars and tasseled sash were perfect. The price was in my discretionary income budget, and, since no vintage fountain pens were in sight, I bought it. I proudly took it home even though it did not fit my top-end weight at the time. With some tonnage reduction the last couple of years, I have shrunk. The lounging jacket now fits. I smile.

Acts 17 has so many misfit stories. Synagogues, market-places, and the Areopagus debate club all had restraints on the Creator's plan for humanity. Jews in the synagogue became jealous of the oversized dimensions of Paul and Silas' God, so they protested the pending upheaval to the civil authority. They would rather call Caesar king and forget the hope for a restoration of David's throne than to open their lives to the Messiah who suffered, died, and rose again. The Jewish leaders from Thessalonica even felt threatened by the Bible study in Berea. Perhaps this oversized God would not stay confined to the city forty-five miles away. The threat rose to a level where the men undertook the two-day journey to stop the God too big for their synagogue.

Berean Jews had scalable faith. If someone opened their understanding of the text, then they searched and studied for themselves. Of course they did this the old school way without Bible study software. Their software was a set of scrolls. Since the Isaiah scroll alone took about thirty-five feet of papyrus, they truly had to search the Scriptures. And they had to search the Scriptures together.

Paul stopped in Athens, the large intellectual center of that part of the world. People still visit the city today and think about its capacity to give space for human thought and art. Its thirty thousand sculptures of gods and heroes seemed to have the capacity to hold any idea, yet it was still too small to hold what God wanted to do for humanity. They sought for truth while God waited nearby.

Athens could not put down their preferred containers to receive God's gifts. They mocked a theology where the Hero died and rose again. The same challenge limits humanity today. Looking back to a golden age of thought, art, heroism, family, or human achievement always leaves a container too small for God. While Jesus people understand that human efforts from yesterday do not fit God's vision, they often shrink God's plans for today by limiting Him to what He has done before. I love to hear the stories of yesterday—of evangelists riding the train or sleeping in their cars. I love to hear of tent meetings and brush arbors. The Azusa Street story still sounds amazing, but those memories are too small for what God wants to do today. If Jesus told His disciples they would do greater works than Him, certainly He says the same today. Greater works will we do than what our grandparents in the faith did. Everything else is too small. We have not gotten any larger or increased our capacity; we just have not reached the limits of the dimensionless God.

My vision just exploded. The only thing I can do now is pray.

---

*Dear Lord,*

*Oh! Your vision for humanity's restoration goes so far beyond my capacity to grasp. In the end, all will be reconciled back to You. My vision sees the anger, division, selfishness, misuse of Your glorious gifts, anxieties, and depression. My study and experiences show the threads of what You are doing, but it is like I used a microscope to zero in on a tiny group of cells rather than seeing the universe of change You want to do.*

*Forgive me, Lord. Sometimes I and my people think the need is to be smarter, work harder, discover new strategies, or market You like You were a new Nike sneaker. Perhaps a bit better, but still inadequate, we think we need to develop some new spiritual discipline that gets You to finally bring an end-time Pentecostal experience our world needs. Forgive me for thinking I am the one who brings Your Spirit to the world. Purify my mouth, my heart, and my hands, I pray. But today I really need my eyes purified.*

*Your purposes will be achieved in the earth, and You have invited Your church to participate by believing and living the message. Like Paul and Silas, I must see the many ways Your death, burial, and resurrection challenge every culture. Our society's containers cannot handle the reality the message conveys. I wonder if I can handle it.*

*Bless us with vision, I pray. Bless Your church with a vision to see both the horrors of our world and the dimensionless wonder of Your grace. You still want to bless those who study Your Word. You still want a church that can speak to hungry Bible study students and to professors like Dr. Dionysius from Athens. But a new shot of faith says You will do as yet unseen things in this hour. Maybe I have wanted to be like the first-century church when You are wanting me to be part of the church today, a church that can see the dimensions of two thousand years of faith and stand ready for what only You can do.*

*I do not need to get out of my box; I need to let You out of the one I have used to constrain You.*

*Is that what it means for Your kingdom to come and Your will to be done? What does that Kingdom look like for nearly eight billion people? My eye has not yet seen, my ear has not yet heard, and my mind has not yet*

*conceived what Your death, burial, and resurrection will*
*do in the human chaos today.*
   *Lord, I believe; please help my unbelief.*
   *In Jesus' name,*
   *Amen*

---

Thank you for walking with me through Acts 17. I know the exploding boundaries of God's kingdom work can leave you a little disoriented as it does me. I pray the Lord gives you the courage to plot your location and mission direction based on His leading rather than the confining boundaries imposed by a broken society.

   God bless,
   Jim

# 42 | A *WALK* THROUGH ACTS 18

I enjoy sitting with my parents and listening to their stories from years gone by. Now that I am in my last years as a pentagenarian, Mom and Dad must go back to the first fourth of their life to uncover yesteryears untouched by the detritus of my own existence. As I listen raptly and probe for more information, I feel like an archeologist peeling back the layers to a strange time.

Not only did Dad grow up without electricity, running water, or a second room in his schoolhouse, they did not travel at all. As I sit on my couch in Texas and reflect on the years gone by, I realize how different my life has been from some of my ancestors just a few generations ago. Our family migration from southern Illinois to upstate New York set the trajectory for my whole life in so many ways. My life highlight reel also includes a wonderful trip with Dad to Taiwan.

As a child, however, Dad only read about strange places like the Florida Everglades. I guess Dad and his two siblings pestered my grandfather enough that he finally acquiesced. Grandad loaded his excited children into the family sedan and headed south . . . all the way to the Arkansas border. Perhaps the forty-five-mile trip took an hour. After crossing the border, he immediately turned around and told them to not ask to travel again. Evidently Grandpa Littles's bucket list was a bit limited when it came to travel. I do not say that with criticism; much of my grandfather's life revolved around surviving and supporting those he loved. Travel required a purpose.

This year I got to do ministry travel from Vancouver, British Columbia, to Indonesia. Past trips have taken me as far south as Buenos Aires, Argentina, north to Dawson City, Yukon, and east to Fukuoka, Japan. Sherri and I have traveled more this past year than we have ever traveled before. Sometimes my bucket list is to stay home for two or three weeks and enjoy the view out my back window.

Now our whole world seems to travel. Cities of any size have various ethnic enclaves. Public transportation and shopping centers tickle the ears with foreign languages and the nose with spices from distant lands. In the olden days, you had to sit in someone's living room to watch the slides from the Mt. Rushmore vacation or their 8mm silent movies of the beach. Now we invite everyone to tell their stories in our own living rooms through Facebook and Instagram.

Humanity now floats around the globe. Sometimes the float becomes a destructive tsunami, but we are always on the move.

Reading Acts 18 reminds me that my church family carries the migratory DNA. It started with a refugee from Ur and threads through Egypt on its way to Palestine where the Illegal Alien was born in a barn. The early church continued this migration lifestyle. The chapter moves around from places like Alexandria, Egypt, to Rome, Corinth, and Ephesus. Apollos doubtlessly traveled with a trunk of scrolls and journals accounting for his time with John the Baptist. Aquila and his wife, Priscilla, would certainly not make it through TSA checkpoints with their tent-making equipment. Paul probably had both scrolls and tools of the trade in his go bag.

The Spirit moved along with the people.

In some places they experienced rejection. When that happened, they shook the dust from their garments and moved on to another audience. Sometimes the audience grew offended and took them to court. While there, the disciples witnessed a brutal hate crime as Sosthenes bled before the disinterested eye of the judge.

Travels happened with the simple clause, "If God wills" (Acts 18:21, ESV). At times the Lord lavishly loved His traveling disciples by comforting them with visions: "Do not be afraid, but go on speaking and do not be silent, for I am with you, and no one will attack you to harm you, for I have many in this city who are my people" (Acts 18:9–10, ESV). At times the disciples disappointed new believers as they traveled to the next city with the promise to return if the Lord willed it to be so. They stayed from a matter of days to a year and a half.

The scenery and foods may have changed, but one thing never changed. God sent them to make disciples in the cities.

Pentecost thrives in urban spaces. Spaces of commerce, manufacturing, and convergence of cultures provide the cityscape of a new work of the Spirit. Spaces of government, banking, intellectual pursuits, and the urban poor cry out for Pentecostal witness. Cities always experience change, and urban change provides the seedbed for the harvest.

Jesus still sends small businesspeople like Paul, Priscilla, and Aquila to the cities. He still sends teachers like Apollos. He still sends visions to reduce the fear and open the eyes to see much people. Unless the church hears the beckoning of the city over the anxiety of her own heart, she will not know the Lord's will. Though cobblestone streets have given way to concrete veins to carry the masses, God's heartbeat can still be heard the loudest in the cities.

I think my grandfather and father would understand this kind of travel, a travel with a goal in mind. The Lord's will be done in confined spaces where stacks of people reach to the heavens.

The cities call me to pray.

*Lord,*

*You had a voice calling in the wilderness before You came the first time. Before You come the second time, I hear the voices calling from the cities. Like farmers plow their fields with nitrogen, phosphorus, and potassium, You have fertilized the world's cities with migrating populations in search of something. You have prepared the soil.*

*Do You still give the burden of unreached cities like You did to Paul and Silas? Is it still possible for men and women to hear urban cries as my mother and father did? The cities have greater needs today than ever before; surely You have a church well prepared for the season of harvest.*

*Lord, would You give us visions and dreams again? Surely You have even more people in Dallas, Houston, and San Antonio than know Your name today. Chicago, LA, Seattle, DC, Miami, New York, Denver, and Phoenix need thousands of more missionaries. Mexico City, London, Paris, Johannesburg, Moscow, Cairo, Mumbai, Tokyo, and Beijing all await the healing wave of witnesses You raise up in this last hour.*

*I am thankful for the missionaries who have gone before with the support of mission-minded churches, but the cites need more! Do you still have any small businessmen and women who can go? Perhaps some who get pushed out of one city with much confusion only to learn this was part of Your will? Do You have any social workers, engineers, educators, urban planners, architects, accountants, web designers, longshoremen, cooks, and office cleaners that You could send to the cities? Can You gift them to love the city when they have receptive ears as well as when they experience hate crimes?*

*I weep because You show me the cities, and I do not know how to pray prayers that big. I weep because I am afraid that we are not ready for the urban Pentecost You have planned for the world.*

*I weep, but I also hope. Just as the winds blow with the changing season outside my window today, Your Spirit blows over the face of the world's cities. Send us. Send me.*

*Oh Lord! "Thy kingdom come, Thy will be done" . . . in the cities.*

*In Jesus' name,*
*Amen*

---

Thank you for walking with me through Acts 18. Do not be afraid of the people streams that flow around you. The Master is up to something overwhelming in all the migration. Listen closely and you will hear the cries around you and the Voice that says you were wonderfully designed for this hour.

God bless,

Jim

# 43 | A *WALK* THROUGH ACTS 19

Keeping track of time has changed quite a bit since Moses wrote, "And the evening and the morning were the first day" (Genesis 1:5). He did not talk about hours, minutes, or seconds—just two halves of the day. Those close to the Tabernacle could use their nose to tell the time by the evening and morning sacrifices. Sundials used shadows to track hours by 3500 BC. Chinese monks and scholars developed the first mechanical clock that used water-driven wheels to beat a drum every quarter hour and ring a bell every full hour (AD 725). By the fifteenth century, the French had clocks with gears and springs rather than using water or weights. Clocks improved to the point where they lost only four minutes per day and would set the stage for miniaturized versions that could be put in a vest pocket. Of course you can now link your watch to your phone to keep track of your steps, heartbeats, and text messages.

Watch collecting has become quite a subculture. One company tried to cater to those who wanted luxury watches but could not afford a closet shelf full of autowinders. For a monthly fee of $149 on the low end to $999 on the upper end, Eleven James would send you a new luxury watch every three months as long as you sent the last one back to them. Imagine leasing watches just like someone leasing a luxury SUV!

As you might guess, I am a mechanical watch guy. While mine were all found for less than one hundred dollars, I enjoy winding them to set a new day in motion. I pick the watch, wind the crown, set the time, and change the date if necessary.

Often I catch myself wanting to control time rather than being satisfied with simply synchronizing my watch. I want to slow down the joyful times with one of the ladies in my life (all princesses—Mom, Sherri, Jen, Amanda, Jane, and Juhina) or my son, James III. Times with Dad become more cherished with each passing year. Grandchildren, from the eldest, Jaden, to the youngest, Jubayr, make time special; distance has made those times even more precious.

Painful times somehow have the power of making time crawl, while approaching deadlines accelerate time. From my experience Einstein was right: time is not very consistent.

One of my human weaknesses expresses itself when I try to alter God's timing. The Bible clearly explains His desire to be with all humanity, and His work in Christ reconciles all things to Himself. He has promised to give us the ministry (deeds) of reconciliation and the words of reconciliation as part of His creation upcycling process. God made the promises; I believe Him.

How long, Oh Lord, will this take? Are we almost there? Why has it taken this long? Millions of saints have prayed, labored, believed, and died, yet the time has not yet come.

Sometimes I catch myself looking at my spiritual clock and wondering if it still works. Surely time seems to have stopped. Perhaps if we scream louder, pray harder, or hunger more, then we could make God's time speed up.

Forgive me, Lord.

Paul disappointed the people of Ephesus in Acts 18. He said he would come back at some later point if the Lord willed. Evidently the Lord's timing brought this to pass in Acts 19. Time was right. The twelve disciples of John the Baptist would now hear of Jesus' name baptism and the Holy Spirit. They spoke in tongues and prophesied; they had only waited twenty years or so! How long had those who experienced "extraordinary miracles" waited (Acts 19:11, ESV)? Why did people have to suffer the manipulation of magical arts and waste so much wealth on the illusion of help or demonic control when God promised to bless all nations through Abraham's children in Genesis 12?

Watches, sundials, and calendars do not capture God's timing. Lifetimes fail as well. When God's timing was right, Ephesus became the center of Kingdom witness to that region of the world.

God's will disrupts more than the normal progress of time. Some responded to the disruption to the time-space continuum with unbelief and speaking evil of the Way. Others threw out valuable investments in magic arts as they saw the Word of the Lord continue to increase and prevail mightily. Those who tried to harness the power for their exorcism business got a beating.

God will always cause confusion and delay for the established order. Actually the disruption comes to the disorder around which people have ordered their lives.

While a silversmith instigated the riot, most agitated people in the arena did not know why they joined the protest. They joined the worship of Artemis (Diana) without a reason. Someone told them to jump, so they did. Someone told them to scream, so they did. Someone told them to shout out the greatness of the Ephesian god; they did so for two hours.

Paul and his team lived a life of worship during the Ephesian chaos. Some people actively rejected them; some people received with joy. Other folks got swept up in the frenzy while a few folks maintained a dispassionate middle ground. Paul's ministry approach spoke powerfully for Christ, but he did not act sacrilegiously or blaspheme other faith systems. Following God's timing gave the disciples peace of mind to proclaim Christ without shaming others. Sometimes city fathers brought riots; at other times thy served as peacemakers while Paul proclaimed the Prince of Peace.

Releasing the need to control or anticipate God's timing frees disciples to do and speak righteousness.

The Word calls me to pray.

---

*Dear Lord,*

*I am a bit weary today, and the coming weeks have more events crowded into them than what I think I can accomplish to my satisfaction. I fear disappointing You, others, and myself. By this time, I thought . . . well, I do not know exactly what I thought, I just know I didn't think my life would look like this.*

*I know much of the exhaustion comes from my own making. You have shown me some of the wonderful things You are doing to reconcile all things to Yourself, and I want to see them come to pass. Then I proudly think I can accelerate the time or make it happen by working harder. Somehow I took the responsibility of getting the mission accomplished. I am sorry for judging Your schedule and faithfulness to Your promises as inadequate. I repent of my pride of thinking I could improve on Your Spirit moving on the face of chaos as You make all things new.*

*Casting all my anxieties on You represents a significant part of my repentance. I humbly do so today. I take my hands off my feeble attempts to control time as if my manipulation of clock hands changes things.*

*I rejoice in the freedom to simply live the Kingdom way. You make living holy and justly possible even when I do not see results on the schedule as I would like to see them. I put down disappointments of missed timetables and rest in the peace and hope You offer. Living as a disciple brings joy whether I see the results today or not. Being renewed daily as part of Your new creation opens my capacity to see new ways You recreate all things. I will simply do what You have put in my hands for today.*

*I breathe again. I breathe more deeply than I did yesterday. I breathe in the freshness of Your Spirit and feel life where I was afraid my bones could not live again. Thank you for helping me to put down my timetable and expectations one more time. My back could not handle the weight; those expectations squeezed the life out of me. Letting You be God and carry the burdens makes me feel alive again.*

*Hallelujah!*

*"Thy kingdom come, Thy will be done" . . . in Your timing.*

*Amen*

---

Thank you for walking with me through Acts 19. I trust the Spirit will call and equip you to walk in God's timing in this season of your life. Do not be afraid of failing to achieve enough to warrant His love. You are loved. Walking in that love will free you to celebrate His faithful timing.

God bless,

Jim

# 44 | A *WALK* THROUGH ACTS 20

"They" begin lying to us as children. Even in kindergarten "they" told us that we could be anything we wanted to be, that all we had to do was dream big and work the plan. What a lie! Some people have mathematical or verbal giftings. Other people have one of the other six forms of intelligences proposed by Howard Gardner. Joseph Renzulli and colleagues developed further models of child giftedness that exploded the number of gifting areas that accounted for differences in interest, style preferences for instruction, learning environment, thinking, and expression. Children are not born with equal abilities and do not get equal opportunities. Gifted behavior happens when a child has above average ability, creativity, and task commitment. Francoys Gagne proposes that one in ten children are moderately gifted while only one in one hundred thousand are extremely gifted.

When will we stop lying to children? When will we stop lying to ourselves?

We cannot be anything we want to be. Without kinesthetic intelligence, another foot in height, and a basketball environment, I could never achieve a goal of being a professional basketball center, much less the best one. Of course, I would have to be a foot shorter, ninety pounds lighter, and comfortable with very small margin of error to win the

Kentucky Derby, assuming I had the right horse. Sadly our culture sets up many people for lifelong disappointment.

Unrealistic expectations often cause marriages to fail and careers to implode. Unrealistic expectations can lead to chronic depression, pressures to perform, anger toward parents and culture that did not set the table for success, and even contemplating suicide when the gap between expectations and current reality remains too wide for too long.

Life is a gift from God! We are all made in His image and blessed with limitations. Limitations allow us to humbly flourish in our personal giftings in the place where we find ourselves. Limitations enable us to join with others as they celebrate their accomplishments and walk alongside others when they suffer failures. Perhaps limitations are one of our greatest gifts.

As I walk through Acts 20, Paul's giftings and limits leap from Luke's quill. This treasured leader encounters so many disciples and elders who want to see the apostle one more time before his appointed end closes in on him. While the chapter has an account of one teaching event and summarizes many others as "in public and from house to house," most of the chapter recounts Paul's gifting as an encourager. Acts 20 has no church plants and only one miracle (necessitated by a young man's inability to stay awake during Paul's lengthy teaching).

Luke captures the multiple dimensions of encouragement as a spiritual gift needed for the church to remain a missionary people. In other places he celebrates exorcising of demons, surviving shipwreck, shaking off snakes, healing the lame, and planting new churches. This chapter does not have that element of apostolic life. Instead the author emphasizes the necessity of the quiet gift of encouragement.

Perhaps encouragement gifting plays such a critical role in a faithful church because true disciples live like Jesus. His powerful mission went through days of prayer, wrestling with

Satan, opposition by the theological crowd and powerbrokers, rejection from dear friends, and violence. Even casual readers must realize the trappings of the "good life" somehow don't find their way into the story.

The realistic goal of living faithfully as a disciple requires encouragement. Distractions of fame and success smoothly insert themselves into my expectation list like rust use to eat through the steel of my cars in New York: from the inside out.

Paul's encouragement came through his words and his lifestyle. In a touching scene in Miletus, where the Ephesian elders met the apostle of encouragement, Paul recounted the walk of humility punctuated with tears and trials from external threats. The encouragement brought memories of walking the path together. Paul's words sowed the seeds for realistic expectations for the years to come. Unfortunately the elders did not fully grasp the dimensions of the encouragement. By the end of the generation, John would record Jesus' words to the church elders—great work, but you lost the first love (Revelation 2:1–7).

The encouraging apostle reminded the elders of his testimony of repentance and faith in the Lord Jesus Christ, a testimony delivered to both Jews and Greeks. He also reminded them of the Holy Spirit's testimony in every city. The Spirit forewarned him of the coming difficulty through personal constraints or feelings as well as through prophets' words everywhere he went. The road to Jerusalem would end with imprisonment and afflictions. Do modern readers really get the juxtaposition of the apostle's testimony given to many against the testimony he received from the Spirit?

Paul confessed his life goal as part of his encouraging words: "If only I may finish my course and the ministry that I received from the Lord Jesus, to testify to the gospel of the grace of God" (Acts 20:24, ESV). He would never see them again, so he left the most encouraging word he could. His life had little value. Being faithful represented the highest estate any disciple could achieve. He could do that, and so could they.

Before the elders accompanied Paul to the ship, the encouraging apostle reset their ministry expectations. The Holy Spirit called them to attend to their own lives and the lives of the flock. Though wolves would come from within, they could remain faithful to the One who is always able to give an inheritance among the saints.

Paul's encouragement reminded the elders of his bivocational ministry. His entrepreneurial skills were applied wherever the Spirit called him. He never expected to be in "full-time" ministry; the encouraging apostle resisted such efforts in his own life while validating ministers who made other choices. The work of Paul's hands supported him and his ministry team; they also provided care for the weak.

The final act of encouragement was to kneel by the docks and pray with the elders.

His encouragement ministry calls me to pray as well.

---

*Dear Lord,*

*Thank You for Your mercies that are new every morning! I so easily default to my old ways of valuing life and things around me. You chose the Cross as the place for me to experience forgiveness and new life. How easily I transform the rugged tree into a piece of silver jewelry that only needs a little daily polishing to look pretty once again. Forgive me for trying to make the Cross look pretty.*

*Thank You for resetting my expectations. You have lifted my eyes today to see eternal expectations rather than a life of leisure and accumulation of treasures. Pursuit of pleasure dies. Quest for faithfulness rises again. Oh, to know the joy of sharing Your grace in times fraught with opposition where the old order tries to stay in power.*

*Today's suffering takes me back to the Cross rather than finding my satisfaction in houses, land, gold, or honor. Today's blessings remind me of the future reality where I join my brothers and sisters and experience the greatest blessing of all—being in Your presence for eternity.*

*Help me to value the apostolic gift of encouragement. For some reason we tend to value times of blazing demonstrative power above quiet, steadfast assurance of the things that really matter. Help me to support others in their encouragement giftings even as I give voice to the encouraging spirit You have placed in me. I look forward to times of kneeling by the docks in prayer as You send all of us on our way.*

*At the docks we will pray, "Thy kingdom come, Thy will be done" in our expectations and demonstration of encouragement power.*

*In Your name,*

*Amen*

---

Thank you for walking through Acts 20 with me. I trust the Spirit's gifting in your life can be felt in a palpable way. Be comforted in your limits as you treasure a life of faithfulness. I look forward to hearing stories of saints in Heaven when they share ways you encouraged them to walk by faith when the way got difficult.

God bless,

Jim

# 45 | A *WALK* THROUGH ACTS 21

Freedom has an intoxicating ring to it. Freedom contains memories of past shackles that have fallen away like a used, unneeded chrysalis. Just saying the word makes me breathe more deeply and experience the wonder of a monochromatic world exploding with thousands of colors.

Freedom speaks of a cost.

"Give me liberty or give me death."

"Don't tread on me."

"I have a dream that one day . . . "

"I have looked over the mountain . . . "

Freedom often speaks of rebellion from an oppressor or a refusal to remain silent in the face of society that invests more in chloroform to restrain those at the margins than to find ways to share freedom with those not like us. Defense systems, prisons, and home protection budgets outpace education and care for the poor.

Wow. That sounded quite liberal.

Why does freedom seldom ring in a way to give up personal prerogatives for the benefit of others? Why does following Jesus to walk in both holiness and care for others get split into opposing camps named conservative and liberal?

As I walk through the frozen images in Acts 21 and pause long enough for the scenes to thaw into moments filled with fresh sights, sounds, smells and emotions, I marvel at the kind of freedom Paul lived. I think the chapter reads like the farewell tour of a beloved family member. Beach ministry looks like gatherings of disciple families who want one last glimpse of the favored uncle. If cell phones were available, then selfies with Paul would rule the day. They had to settle for one more prayer meeting. Those in attendance would never forget those shared moments kneeling by the docks as the Spirit blew more powerfully than the ocean winds.

The Spirit spoke at every stop on the farewell tour. The tenor of the Spirit's words sounded differently to Paul than it did to others. At every harbor, in every hospitable home, in every conversation, the Spirit said bondage awaited Paul at the end of his journey. Jerusalem, the city that loved tombs of dead prophets more than the words of living ones, awaited with chains.

The Spirit spoke in Tyre and in Caesarea. He spoke through Philip's four daughters and through Agabus. Some used object lessons to make the words more concrete. Evidently the Spirit's words left room for interpretation. The well-wishers used the Spirit's words to try to dissuade Paul from going to Jerusalem. They punctuated their words with sobs. They broke Uncle Paul's heart because he understood the Spirit's words differently. Paul heard the Spirit asking if he was ready for prison or even death.

Paul expressed his freedom in saying yes.

The family members grudgingly stopped asking for a different itinerary and acquiesced to the Lord's will.

Frequently freedom's bell sounds differently than what we anticipated.

Paul freely went to Jerusalem. He freely met the brothers one day and the elders the next. He freely gave an update and heard the concerns of the HQ Jewish church—concerns based on rumors that he worked to get Jewish Christians to stop following their traditions. He freely refrained from defending himself. He even went beyond paying for his own vow in the Temple to pay for four others' purification rituals as well.

Paul was truly free. He had already met his Defender on the Damascus Road and accepted the offered freedom three days later. He taught liberty from Jewish traditions when preaching to the Gentiles, and he lived the liberty to bring peace to a nervous Jewish church in Jerusalem.

He got beat up for his freedom.

Luke gives no evidence that he blamed James for the nervous rule keepers. He was free.

He was free to walk in chains.

He was free to accept momentary deliverance at the hand of pagan soldiers.

He used his freedom to testify one more time.

The Spirit speaks again. I think I need to kneel with Uncle Paul and my family and pray by the beach.

---

*Dear Lord,*

*Thank you for doing all You did to make my freedom possible. You led the way on Freedom Trail by choosing to drink from the cup, resisting the urge to beckon thousands of angels who gazed with astonishment as You left bloody footprints up that hill, and by letting love hold You to the tree.*

*You freed me from the wages of sin and death. You freed me, so I could hear Your voice and live as a freedom witness.*

*Forgive me of the times I've used freedom to satisfy my desires, try to get even with someone, or doubted when the Freedom Trail takes me through rugged places. I deeply value the examples Uncles Paul and Peter posted on the Freedom Trail. I've seen signs left by many other travelers as well. Because of them, I walk today.*

*Lord, I treasure Your love for me and my big family more than ever before. Could You speak to us again? Could You give us the strength to face tomorrow? Can You help us respect and value those who can only muster a whispered "God's will be done"?*

*Finally, we want to pray, "Thy kingdom come, Thy will be done, in earth as it is in heaven," by respecting both rule keepers and new converts from different cultures. Be glorified as we walk freely toward one more testimony opportunity—even when we do so in chains.*

*In Jesus' name,*

*Amen*

---

Thank you for walking with me through the Freedom Trail in Acts 21. I'm sure the Lord has powerful plans for you today and tomorrow. Walk boldly as one set free for such a time as this. You are free to respond to circumstances in light of the Spirit rather than reacting to difficult situations you may encounter.

God bless,

Jim

# 46 | A *WALK* THROUGH ACTS 22

I must confess, I do not understand many things that go on in the world around me. I do not understand the fascination with torn jeans worn by people who could afford a pair with years of wear in them. Another thing that puzzles me is the way passion finds its way into so many discussions. People cook with passion, sing with passion, and design widgets with passion. Perhaps living in a time of relative affluence sets the stage for many people in my country to look for passion to decide what they will do with their life. Just saying the word makes them feel set apart, special. Public discourse seems to say being passionate about something should guarantee success and acclaim from those who matter. If a person can't be passionate about something, then become passionate about someone who is passionate.

Passion for passion provides the fuel for a world gone mad for celebrity. We wear clothes with other people's names on them—a clear mark of being owned by someone with passion. The youngest self-made billionaire comes from a family that is famous for being famous. Their lives become a reality show. The reality show created a need to be like those people, so the young lady had a ready-made market for her clothing line. While I do not understand reality shows, I must admit the young lady is quite brilliant in harnessing a world's need for the next best thing to passion . . . dressing like someone who has "it."

As I walk through Acts 22, I see a story filled with passion. Reading the story reminds me of pictures of a girl touching a static electricity ball in a children's science museum. The electricity makes her hair literally stand on end. The air carried a similar charge as Paul began to defend himself. Passion ran wild on all sides.

Paul began his defense as many speakers do today. He presented his credentials as a favored son. He had passionately studied at the feet of the greatest teacher of the day and used his education to zealously hunt down the people of the Way who threatened the foundation of Jewish identity. Like modern-day Mossad members who hunted down Nazi war criminals or the 1972 terrorists that assassinated eleven Israeli summer Olympic athletes in Munich, Paul tracked down followers of the Christ in ever-widening concentric circles. The elders could witness to this man's zeal for God and the warrants he carried to Damascus.

True zeal or passion acts on behalf of some cause. Once Saul found out who blinded him on his mission to Damascus, he asked what Jesus wanted him to do. He had to surrender his purpose to arrest people of the Way to hear what he should do. Later in the story, Paul told of times when he received his direction straight from the Lord; his first steps came through a disciple who knew the Law as he did. Ananias greeted his new brother with the new commission: Paul now lived to witness of all the things he had seen and heard.

Perhaps the new job seemed a step down from the old commission. Hunting down faith offenders sure seems more manly than just living to tell the things you have seen and heard. Then again, I suppose that depends on what the witness has seen.

Paul became a part of the great cloud of witnesses. Sometimes they would not accept his testimony. At other times, masses converted from their previous passion to their new passion to become witnesses in their own right.

Most men like shiny things, fast things, and loud things. Handguns and sports cars fascinate us for some reason. Dodge Hellcats and Bass Pro Shops provide evidence that a substantial number of us don't outgrow our boyhood ways. What we cannot have we admire in the possession of others and dream of a ten-car garage or a ten-point buck.

Paul's passion grew beyond a juvenile faith. He did not talk of the miracles of the dead raised, the lame that walked, or servant girls freed from demons. Instead, he took the risk of underscoring the most powerful witness at his disposal. His testimony reached its climax when he recounted the vision when the Lord sent him to witness to the Gentiles.

Reading the story in my recliner makes me seriously question Paul's skill as a litigator. He took that which gave him credentials at the beginning of the witness, zeal for exclusively Jewish faith, and reversed its polarity in a way that gave his audience emotional whiplash. What was he thinking? If he just edited the story in a way that highlighted faithfulness to the Law, then he would have been home in time for dinner. Instead he fulfilled his passion. He witnessed to the wonder of a gospel that invited *all* to experience redemption. In one of his letters, he explained the way Jesus Christ pulled down old categories that created privilege (male or female, Jew or Greek, and free or slave). A gospel that removes all personal privilege is stronger than a gospel that only heals blind eyes, straightens limbs, and survives storms.

Oops, I think Paul is witnessing to me today rather than to the mob. He abandons his credentials as a missionary, preacher, writer, and miracle worker for the simple, yet profound, office as witness. Could discipleship really be that basic? Am I willing to turn away from pursuing the shiny evidence of the Kingdom for the power to witness? Are Acts 22 and Acts 1:8 really true?

Such questions call me to pray.

---

*Dear Lord,*

*I must confess I quest for the shiny parts of the gospel. I know You do many miracles today, and I so want to see more of them. But today the Word calls me to see the greater power in pointing toward the reconciling door that Your deeper, more eternal work will accomplish.*

*I repent of my tendency to put the emphasis in the wrong places. You promised these signs should follow those who believe. You did not call us to seek them or follow them. Instead You strip my power to the one place where I can actually have a voice. You call me and my people to celebrate the wonder of witness: seeing, believing, living, and telling the story of Your eternal life offered to all.*

*Some witnesses will end like Stephen. Other witnesses fade quickly from the plot line like Ananias. Still other witnesses become the focal point of the mission like Paul. But all have that divine power to witness.*

*Could You help me see that power to witness is enough? It seems like You send me as a little boy facing deadly force with a toy rock slinger. But as I think of it, that is exactly what You frequently do. You send us as a sheep among wolves. You send us with no extra resources. You just send us with the words of Emmanuel.*

*I believe the witness is enough. Now I want to live like it.*

*Maybe then I can more honestly pray, "Thy kingdom come, Thy will be done . . . " When I pray that way, I am more satisfied to witness of Your goodness to someone*

*than having the "credit" for healing blind eyes. I pray it*
*again, "Thy kingdom come, Thy will be done."*
  *In Jesus' name,*
  *Amen*

---

Thank you for walking with me through Acts 22. Thank you for being a living witness, a testimony "read" by everyone who encounters you. I pray your greatest delight comes from the simple act of sharing the wonder of being God's son or daughter.

  God bless,
  Jim

# 47 | A *WALK* THROUGH ACTS 23

I had the opportunity to stay at my parents' house in southeastern Missouri on a recent trip to St. Louis. Every visit ignites thanksgiving in my spirit for one more time of fellowship with the best parents anyone could ever have. When I examine my life, I see sparkling treasures that result from growing up in their home, watching their ministry through the years, and now observing tenacious faith in this season of their life.

My brothers and I grew up in a literature-rich environment. Books were everywhere! As a young child in Galatia, Illinois, I remember getting the monthly cardboard box from a book of the month club. When money got a little tight, Mom wrote a note to cancel the order. She let me take it to the post office a few blocks away. I had to struggle a little to get it into the mailbox; for some reason they had it turned to face the wall behind the post office. Since Dad always told us that "can't never could," I found a way to get it into the hard-to-reach opening and shove the letter down the rusted blue mailbox's throat.

I got another book the next month . . . and the next. That is when Mom found out I had deposited the cancelation notice in a discarded mailbox. I like to think I was innocent of any intent to thwart Mom's purse-string tightening. Thinking of the story as I look at one of my bookcases this morning, I do have to smile about the fifty-year-old memory.

Books let me travel to distant places. How many frequent-flyer miles I must have racked up as I read through the *World Book Encyclopedia* set during one of my forced times of rest that kept me from elementary school. Those green-and-white leatherette bound volumes were gifts from Uncle Mel to his home missionary nephews.

On the trip home I got to sift through the downsizing stacks that Mom and a couple of brothers had made the previous week. I found an old copy of *Uncle Tom's Cabin* that still sheltered a postcard from the one-cent-stamp days. I did not hesitate to add three clothbound volumes of *The Happy Hollisters*—I had traveled with them on many adventures as a child. I am sure I reread each book many times. The spines carry the wounds of my carelessness, many moves, and years of abandonment in basement boxes.

Those books told a story. They had a point. Mysteries and history books alike wove the silken sentence threads into a picture to keep a little boy's interest. As an old guy now, I have moments of reflection when I wonder if many of life's stories have a point. Sometimes life seems like a poorly constructed narrative with too many conjunctions and no coherent purpose.

When I first read through Acts 23, I thought I was in one of those pointless stories. I know Luke only had a limited amount of space in the scroll allocated to the ongoing work of the Messiah in the life of His church, so why would he tell a story with no new church or fiery revival? Where is that celebratory refrain, "and the Lord added to the church"? Isolated as it is in the thirty-five verses, nothing significant seems to happen. I am tempted to combine my stroll through this chapter with the next chapter or two, so I can get to the point of Luke's narrative.

In the same way, I often want to fast forward through days or even seasons of my own life when very little plot advancement seems to take place. No one would want to read about this week, month, or quarter of the year. Nothing movie-script-worthy has happened. Frankly, days slip by where I do not know if anything is even Instagram-worthy. Maybe that is why I do not have an account on that social media outlet.

Paul's life had plenty of excitement in chapter 23, but the activity tended to be the survival type. He fanned the flames of disagreement between Pharisees and Sadducees to escape pending doom; Luke had to explain the finer points of the argument because most of his readers would not understand why the courtroom got so heated. A late-night horseback ride with a couple hundred armed guards would get the blood pumping to be sure, but the ride served to relocate the apostle from one stockade to another. He escaped one plot only to be placed in the hand of another unjust judge. I suppose protective custody provided a little more comfort than the welcome planned by the forty vigilantes that had placed a curse on themselves.

In the middle of religious and secular politics, Paul had a God moment: "The following night the Lord stood by him and said, 'Take courage, for as you have testified to the facts about me in Jerusalem, so you must testify also in Rome.'" (Acts 23:11, ESV). Hmm, chapter 23 does have purpose.

Like Joshua, about to take God's people across Jordan, Paul needed the call to be courageous. The God encounter transforms meaningless chaos into a life filled with purpose. Paul would get to witness in Rome, though the journey would have more twists and turns than direct movement. Paul would get to witness in Rome regardless of the natural, human, and spiritual obstacles he would encounter. He had a reason for cold nights in prison and the saddle sores from the midnight ride. He had a point to his story.

It is time for a God encounter that happens in prayer.

*Dear Lord,*

*Sometimes my life story has definition and purpose. In those moments I have no question that the discipleship journey makes sense and all of my labors are not in vain. At other times I lose the plot behind my life. More misdirection and threats to my service fill those weeks and months than evidence of good stewardship.*

*Thank You for the record of Your people. If Joshua and Paul needed words of courage in uncertain times, then perhaps I am in good company. I know that I heard from You again on September 25 this year. In the dream You reminded me that You have a work for Sherri and me. You reminded me that all parts of Your body play a significant role in Your work to reconcile all things to Yourself. You gave me enough detail to know my story fits in Your kingdom plot.*

*Forgive me of the despair I feel when I lose the plot and try to help You fix the story. You have spoken. I have heard. Your stewardship of Paul's life and my life is without question. Your stewardship of all my brothers' and sisters' lives is without question. We are in Your story. You are the author and finisher of our faith. I pray for our courage to face chaotic as well as clearly productive times in the same way . . . by trusting You.*

*Today I sense the courage it takes to pray, "Thy kingdom come, Thy will be done." You have spoken courage into our lives. Your call to be courageous reminds us that our old nature will question our place in the story from time to time. As courageous disciples we will trust You.*

*In Jesus' name,*
*Amen*

Thank you for walking with me through Acts 23. I pray you experience a God encounter this week as you mediate on His word, pray, worship, serve others, and find rest. Such God encounters give us the courage to stay in the story even when we cannot see the plot.

God bless,

Jim

# 48 | A *WALK* THROUGH ACTS 24

When I listen to the words of traditional lullabies, I marvel that children can sleep at all. "Rock-a-bye Baby in the Tree Top" calls for nightmares of falling to the ground. Such unsafe cradle standards certainly would drive all little ones to snuggle in the safety of their parents' bed.

But then again parents' beds might not be safe either. "Peter, Peter, Pumpkin Eater" certifies the longstanding potential of infidelity. Or both parents could lose their heads like French monarchs as commemorated by Jack and Jill's misadventure in falling down the hill with broken crowns.

Nursery rhymes add the reality of taxes to death's certainty. "Baa, Baa, Black Sheep" reminds kids of IRS predecessors that took one bag of wool for the king, one bag for the church, and only left one bag for the farmer.

One explanation for "Ring around the Rosie" places the rhyme and its circle dance in one of the plagues that brought devastation to Europe. Proponents of that origin suggest the ring was the beginning signs of the plague and the ashes represented the end when bodies were cremated to stop the diseases' spread. "Pockets full of posies" could have been an early form of essential oils to ward off the illness or at least the smells of death.

Walking through Acts 24 demonstrates that responses to the gospel's good news are not always positive. The chief priests' hired mouthpiece sought a restraining order against Paul's plague. Freedom from legalism of Pharisees and political and economic exploitation of the Sadducees threatened to bring death to Jewish life as they knew it. Current circumstances under Roman control brought more comfort than the unknown outcome of following the "sect of the Nazarenes" (Acts 24:5). Flattering the despotic Roman governor, a ruler who used both legal crucifixion and hired assassins to destroy hundreds of opponents, brought more hope to Paul's accusers than the Way Paul preached.

Auditing the court proceedings nearly two thousand years later, I am fascinated with Paul's defense. He wonders how his week in Jerusalem could have caused such havoc for them. As a pilgrim seeking to give an offering in the Temple, Paul had only been in the holy city for a few days; the rest of the twelve days he spent in protective custody. He had a clean conscience; they apprehended him in a simple purification ritual rather than in defiling the Temple. Without evidence, they only offered rumor and innuendoes from Asian Jews who did not come to the trial.

Paul did not limit his court time to defending his position. He had the floor, so he used it to witness. He believed every hearing was an opportunity to spread the "plague" of the Way. His worship fulfilled the true directives of the Law and prophets. Once Paul heard the Damascus Road voice, his perspective of worship underwent a radical transformation. He went from policing worship conformity to witnessing worship. Only by living on the mission could the Jesus plague spread.

Paul's conversations with the unjust judge demonstrated his willingness to show people the way of living when they asked. Felix brought his young, beautiful Jewish wife to the first private conference with the apostle. Paul may have known that Felix had seduced her away from her first husband. The scene sounds similar to John the Baptist calling Herod to model righteous living. Paul reasoned about righteousness, self-control, and the coming judgment. Paul must have had a bad case of the plague to confront a governor known for keeping executioners busy.

Luke does not give much information on how Paul spent those two years. Protective custody must have chafed a man of action. Yet he held conferences with the governor when requested and rejected the option of buying his way out of confinement. He must have truly believed the Lord could use these limiting circumstances to achieve Kingdom purposes.

No human-designed strategic plan would suggest prison was a good place for a church planter. No human would use holiness in public service and personal self-control as a witnessing tool. I wonder if I have a full-blown case of the Jesus plague or a nice little inoculation?

The question calls me to prayer.

---

*Dear Jesus,*

*You lived to fulfill the Father's will in everything You did. I can only imagine how much fun You had at times—seeing the blind healed and the dead raised must have been a blast. Passing out wonder bread must have made Your eyes sparkle. But You did it out of faithfulness rather than pursuit of fun. Wrestling with Satan in Your depleted forty-day fast state must have required total focus. That focus took You to the people at the margins where they felt discarded by people of value. In the Olive Press Garden, You prayed for the strength to drink the bitter cup.*

*I repent of the ways I allow even small things to sidetrack my attention. You and Paul went to court, prison, and death for the Kingdom. Sometimes I whine because I need a new fence for my yard or my convertible top is broken. I believe You are calling me to a full-blown case of the Plague, of walking in the Way where small irritants as well as potential satisfaction with "normal" American living fade away with the quest to be faithful.*

*Bless me with focus, I pray. Let that focus guide my actions, emotions, and relationships. That kind of Kingdom focus would provide the guide for daily faithfulness rather than frustration preoccupation. That focus would help me resist buying my way out of challenging circumstances; instead I could worship You at all times. That focus would give me confidence to keep walking when I do not see any progress toward Your kingdom goals.*

*I feel contentment flooding my spirit right now as I pray, "Thy kingdom come, Thy will be done." I know the Spirit will guide me in the refocusing ways you call me to live over the next few months.*

*In Jesus' name,*
*Amen*

---

Thank you for walking with me through Acts 24. Being labeled a person with a one-track mind is not a good thing in our world. Following Jesus with only one thought—to give Him glory in witness and service—redeems living with a singular focus. I pray the Lord blesses you richly this week as you walk the faith path the Master has laid out for you.

God bless,
Jim

# 49 | A *WALK* THROUGH ACTS 25

When I travel beyond the borders of the US, my favorite activity is to take a walk. For example, an unscheduled Saturday in Buenos Aires, Argentina, let me sample the city firsthand. I found the abundance of sidewalk cafes and stationery stores a pleasant surprise. On the other hand, the red tape involved in mailing letters to my grandsons in the US perplexed me to no end. A flight delay once gave Sherri and me a chance to spend an evening walking around Hong Kong before resuming our journey to Singapore. Seeing, smelling, hearing, tasting, and feeling a world-class city can happen on an impromptu walking tour. I value the speed of mass transportation, but I cannot get the same experience while going 60 mph on a bus or 180 mph on a Japanese bullet train.

Once in a while I walk through my hometown as well. The experience does not capture my attention or imagination. Everything is so familiar. But strolling through crowds with different cadences to their speech, speed of walking, and snack preferences serves to highlight differences. Home, well, just feels like home.

I remember reading Washington Irving's "Rip Van Winkle" tale when I was a child. Rip, a Dutch American in New York's Catskill Mountains, awoke after a twenty-year nap to find that his musket stock had been worm-eaten, his beard had grown, and the colonies had transformed into a new country. For a while Rip felt like he lived in a strange country, but once he got over the changes, he resumed his lifestyle of idleness under the care of his daughter.

Walking through Acts 25 gives me a strange feeling of familiarity with a twist. The feeling is not unlike a walking tour of Singapore where they speak English and use dollars. Accents, mannerisms, history, and customs differ, but so much looks similar. Of course, I am not minimizing the differences one might experience in the pristine city with its strict laws and driving on the "wrong" side of the road. I am sure Caesarea offered sights and smells far different from my world, but I also notice several similarities with my world. These similarities beckon me to refocus on my city as a place in need of a missionary witness.

Paul's trials occurred in a world of pragmatic pluralism. The Roman Empire provided a marketplace for spiritualities. The Pantheon of Greek and Roman gods had room to include regional gods of conquered people. Jews could maintain their monotheism since they had an ancient religion and offered no threat to other gods or the growing Caesar cult. Rome just wanted peace where the Empire could prosper, expand, and ward off threats that came from the frontiers. Those who upset this balance of peace would be severely punished.

My pragmatic world worships at the temple of tolerance as well. Contemporary American society encourages people to create their own spiritual hybrids. Morality then as now focuses on accepting all ideas; immorality often gets redefined as questioning another person's truth. All other human behavior would be adiaphora—that is, spiritually and morally neutral. Politics, power, and currying favor with various interest groups becomes the "good" thing to do.

Festus represents the desire to find favor with others through political manipulation of events. Paul's accusers wanted a favor from the governor, and he wanted to do them a favor. Festus also wanted to stay in favor with King Agrippa, the king's sister Bernice, and the emperor in Rome. In order to do so, he had to navigate the existing legal structures of the day. Festus crafted his story in a way that made his administration look good.

In Acts 25 Luke set the stage for Paul's defense testimony in the next chapter. The setting juxtaposes Paul and King Agrippa's characters. Paul stood with his few supporters. The apostle already knew God had ordered his steps to go to Rome. He refused to live his days avoiding death. If he was legally convicted of true accusations, then he would accept the resulting death sentence. He would reject charges of desecrating the Temple. He would accept charges of following his resurrected Lord. As we will see in chapter 26, Paul would turn the trial into one more missionary activity rather than seeking to satisfy pragmatic pluralism policies.

On the other hand, we see the pomp and circumstance around King Agrippa and his sister. Just a decade or so before, their father's life ended in the same city when he declared his own greatness (Acts 12:23). Paul's hearing provided another opportunity for the king to parade his tribunes and their soldiers through the city streets. The clanging of swords, shuffle of combat sandals, and thunder of the officers' mounts carried the king's authority into the courtroom. As many as five thousand armed soldiers and prominent men of the city created quite a spectacle.

The young king needed all of this to bolster his newly expanded authority. The apostle only saw an open door to follow the Spirit's prompting.

The stark differences between these two sources of power call me to prayer.

*Lord,*

*I marvel again at the Incarnation! You came into this world to transform it through serving and suffering. You did not declare judgment from Your magisterial throne. You still send Your people as incarnational missionaries into this world.*

*I confess that social changes over the last couple of decades often confuse me. I lament my country's steps away from a form of Christianity. I acknowledge my fears and uncertainties over those changes. I realize it was largely a form of godliness without any power. The loss highlights the need for missionary living once more. I repent of triumphal forms of the church where we think civil power, political prominence, and visible evidence of defeating all other thought forms serve as evidence that "we" are winning.*

*Help me follow You and Paul. Help me to go into a confused, pluralistic world that has so little hope of finding real peace and healing. You still send Your people without extra purses and as sheep among the wolves. Expand my vision again to value the Spirit's power in sending us rather than leaning on political, financial, or military power. Walking in the Spirit is never weak.*

*Finally, I want to find more comfort in sharing Your name again to a pluralistic society than in avoiding pain or even death that political forces may impose. My place is in service. I never want to feel at home here again. Thank you for awakening me from my slumber.*

*As we pray "Thy kingdom come, Thy will be done," You will give us the strength to awaken from slumber, to see stark differences between Your kingdom and this world, and retain our missionary identity rather than seeking comfort and coexistence in the pluralistic marketplace of ideas.*

*We can only do this through Your Spirit as we live out*
*this mission as one people.*
*In Jesus' name I pray,*
*Amen*

---

Thank you for walking with me through Acts 25. As you walk through your world this week, remember that you are a stranger sent on a mission from the King. Your world elevates personal power and privilege. In contrast, your humble walk of serving as a witness flows from your relationship with the King supreme. Know the King has gifted you and sent you for this time.

God bless,

Jim

# 50 | A *WALK* THROUGH ACTS 26

I have been a defendant at court only one time in my life. To say I did not enjoy the process would be an understatement. I could have settled the situation out of court, but in my mid-twenties justice captured my emotions and decision-making processes more than pragmatic concerns. I felt like I was the victim rather than the perpetrator, so I wanted my day in court. Even thirty-five years later I am still a bit bugged by the incident.

The drama started late one night on the way home from the Busti Fire Department where a brother or two served on the volunteer roster. My first and only motorcycle—a 1974 Honda 450, if memory serves me correctly—was beneath me, and my friend Kyle held on for dear life behind me. The country lane from Busti to my parents' home in Jamestown, New York, could probably accommodate two automobiles passing one another, but it did not have the room for my bike, its passengers, and an Alaska Malamute dog. Something had to give.

While I truly feel sorry for the dog, I give thanks for the guardian angel that fought to keep the bike upright and both passengers astride. As a relatively inexperienced biker, I could hardly believe my good fortune. I had trouble breathing as well. We made it to our destination without further incident, even though the bike needed a little work before I could shift gears again.

The dog did not move. Cops were called. One of my beloved brothers outed me. I got a summons to appear in court to face the charge of leaving the scene of an injured dog. Who knew that was even on the books! Evidently Busti's justice of the peace feared I was a flight risk, so I had to post sixty dollars bail. I could have just paid the $20 fine, but I wanted justice. The dog attacked me where I minded my own business on the public thoroughfare.

Two weeks later I lost my case. I listened to the JP's tirade that he could not level a heaver fine. He also threated to start all investigations involving biker violence at my parents' house where the cop saw four of the dangerous rigs. After I got my forty dollars refund, the judge left his bench to shake hands with the grieving dog owners. He must have been up for reelection.

In hindsight, I should have asked for a jury trial—the judge rigged my case!

Walking through Acts 26 I see a completely different attitude in the defendant's heart. Paul's ability to keep himself out of the center of the story astounds me. After the show of force we saw in chapter 25, the apostle acted like . . . well, he acted like an apostle. For someone on Christ's mission, every event looks like an opportunity to share God's goodness. Paul knew the potential outcomes of the trial; after all, he explained that he had served as the prosecutor on a few cases just like this.

I find Paul's statement of charges quite fascinating. He explained to the gathered dignitaries that his primary crime was hope. I thought I got a bum rap for leaving the scene of an injured dog; Paul faced the charge of having hope.

I wondered if I could get convicted of that one. Would my accusers find enough evidence of hope to keep the circuit court's interest long enough to hear the case?

With the charge clarified, Paul astutely argued his case. If he occupied the center of the case, then the defense would be around his actions. Since his hope came from above, Paul served as a witness for the One who brought him hope. The Old Testament promised hope; Jesus delivered it. Would the circuit court find Paul guilty of receiving this eternal hope that the dead would rise?

Paul's first exhibit for the defense was his old life of fury. He pursued, persecuted, and affirmed the death penalty for other people who followed Jesus. His greatest hope at that time was to see someone blaspheme their Savior. Instead he had to hear people like Stephen intercede on his behalf. Hope replaced fury.

Paul used his conversion story as his second exhibit. Each time Paul told his story it looks a little different. He focused the details on the audience. They *had* to feel his condition, perplexity, and finally joy in conversion. After all, that is what a witness does: he tells of his experience.

The commission as servant and witness made up the third exhibit. This piece of evidence could play a critical role in proving he truly lived in hope. Some could offer counterevidence that shipwrecks, beatings, prison deprivations, and loss of status made joy impossible. Paul insisted he joyfully lived to serve and witness regardless of any given day's incidentals.

Paul finished his argument with his strongest evidence. His joy came alive when he saw the light and liberty God offered to all people. Not only could they repent of sinful ways, but they could also actually live like liberated people! Paul explained how witnessing the power to change triggered his arrest. He ought to know. He had arrested others for witnessing to the same power.

As I look over the trial transcript, I think Paul left out some key evidence. Yet again he did not talk about raising people from the dead, casting out demons, or healing the sick. Miracles would not convict him of having hope. He had learned the lesson of the seventy witnesses in Luke 10. Jesus taught them to find joy in having their name in the Book rather than making demons obey their command. Paul and the seventy had power, but power did not bring them joy. Witnessing did.

No wonder Festus said Paul was out of his mind. The prisoner should not have such hope.

My goodness, the hope-filled prisoner's case calls me to pray.

---

*Dear Lord,*

*You know I am a checklist kind of guy. I put celebrating simple joy on my list for this week. You also know my basic personality resides on the melancholy side. My personality interacts with the gifts You give me to see spiritual things; this can be an explosive combination. I see people in Scripture as well as in the contemporary world who suffer from more depression than joy in certain seasons of their lives. I repent of looking for joy in wrong places. I confess of seasons of emotional unholiness—emotions controlled by circumstances rather than faith and true hope.*

*I pray for the kind of hope Paul modeled. I confess I want that more than I want things to go my way. I confess my longing to recenter all things in my life around You and Your mission. You have already fulfilled Your promises. You have already determined the end of the age when all things are restored to You. That fills me with hope. That kind of hope brings the transformation of my emotions and my purpose.*

*I reposition signs of Your power to the position of following me as a believer rather than something I pursue. Miracles and other faith outcomes cannot bring lasting change in my emotions. Instead, I know You have saved me, transformed me, and commissioned me to be a missionary witness with all of Your people. You took me through strange paths in my life, but these paths simply reveal Your goodness in many ways. Thank You for this seedbed of hope and joy. I harvest it today. I live today in the wonder of being Your son—the wonder of sharing Your eternal goodness with others.*

*When I pray, "Thy kingdom come, Thy will be done," I do so through the hope of seeing that Kingdom unfold around me. Thank You for eyes to see, ears to hear, and a heart to feel the outbreaking of Your kingdom. I delight in witnessing about the Kingdom unfolding right in front of me.*

*In Jesus' name,*
*Amen*

---

Thank you for walking through Acts 26 with me. I pray our stroll through Paul's trial transcript has called you to hope—a hope rooted in God's completed purposes when His kingdom has fully come. Go ahead, smile and dance a little as you celebrate and witness your hope before the world. I trust there is enough evidence to convict you of the hope charge.

God bless,
Jim

# 51 | A *WALK* THROUGH ACTS 27

An ever-changing world requires a shifting skill set. Children now take keyboarding classes in early elementary school, but many never learn to read or write cursive. In many ways I lament the loss of handwriting. This morning I used a vintage Conway Stewart 58 to jot a few notes. People wonder why I paid one hundred dollars for the pen ten years ago. I often hear comments about how many plastic Bics they can buy for that amount. My pen is cheaper, lasts far longer, and brings me more writing pleasure than the three or four phones I have had during that period.

I am not against phones; they do come in handy for checking email, fidgeting while waiting for Sherri to come out of Wal-Mart, and finding directions. I no longer have an atlas in the car or a glove box full of maps from various states. Those big, accordion-folded sheets of paper that mapped all the arteries of American transportation languish in antique stores with the fountain pens. Now men who would never admit they are lost or pause to ask for directions take orders from a lady every time they go off the beaten path. While GPS may take me through parts of town I may not have gone on my own, I do not get lost anymore. I only miss the old maps when Sherri and I want a "wandering vacation" where we keep to three rules: stay off four-lane highways, avoid bad weather, and turn around when half the money runs out.

As I walk through Acts 27, I am struck by the way Paul was literally and figuratively swept away by the currents of life. Other people decided when they would leave one port for another, the type of ship they would ride, and when they would pause for wintering. Paul gave suggestions, but no one paid attention to the prisoner.

The trip began on small coast-hugging boats, but they soon switched to a ship transporting grain from Egypt to the masses in Rome. The ship owner and captain had to balance the threat of a late-season voyage against profits to be earned. The decision to leave Fair Haven made sense; they left a city without a safe harbor for Phoenix where the ship would find protection from storms from any direction. They could certainly take the risk to sail for one more day to reach a safe place to winter.

The day began with a gentle breeze. Then the northeastern winds blew off the seven-thousand-foot mountaintops and the sea became angry. Sailors threw some of the cargo and equipment overboard rather than the preacher, as had happened so many years ago. This preacher experienced sustaining grace rather than delivering grace. Luke did not record rebuking of the storm or crying out for deliverance. Paul had not chosen the destination or set the course. His deep-seated confidence in the One who called him to witness before kings sustained him through the sunless days.

Paul predicted loss, "not only of the cargo and the ship, but also of our lives" (Acts 27:10, ESV). He may have felt anxious over the decisions others had made. Luke drove the point home by stating, "All hope of our being saved was at last abandoned" (Acts 27:20, ESV). Paul had defended his hope when threatened by human adversaries in chapter 26; now his hope suffered with this new threat. As the storm screamed of pending death and the arms of the sea reached up to receive the bodies of those about to die, Paul experienced fear with the other 275 people on the ship. The clouds blocked any hope of mapping the journey by plotting a course with the stars.

But the heavens were not silent.

At that moment Paul got a messenger from God. The angel commanded him to reject the rational fear of the moment in favor of the deep confidence in God's call so many years ago. The wind could change nothing. While sailors bound the ship with ropes to try to keep the boards secure, Paul held himself together by the angel's reminder that he would stand before the king. He did not pray against the storm; he already had a word that the storm would pass.

Paul got a bonus message—he got to keep all the people on the ship from harm too.

The storm provided a convincing background for Paul to witness yet again. He spoke of the One he worshiped, the One who sent the messenger. Paul may have lost hope of surviving the storm prior to the angelic visit, but he kept his faith. That kind of faith must be shared with a world that can only trust in fragile, eggshell-like lifeboats in those dark stormy nights. After the witnessing came the food for those who had fasted for fourteen days.

That kind of faith calls me to pray.

---

*Dear Jesus,*

*My world needs real faith—a faith that can speak in those dark, hopeless nights. I am ashamed of moments when I have lost hope that the storms will pass. I know You have called Sherri and me to serve You with our lives, but a few of the storms seem to have lasted so long that our efforts and voices seem to be lost in the chaos.*

*Thank You for the Bible's honesty. Paul defended his hope in one chapter when faced with a king and five thousand soldiers, but in the storm his hope wavered. You did not abandon him in those moments. Instead You chose to send him a message.*

*Thank You for all the messages You have sent my way through the years. Some messages have come through dreams and a vision. Other messages came through a dear saint sharing a word with me that had originated in Your throne room.*

*I have confidence that Sherri and I will make it through every storm to come, just as You have taken us through so many in the past. Give me the courage to know when to quit praying against the storm and start sharing faith with people who are so terrified and hungry in the storm. Help me to trust Your guiding hand when life seems to give me very few options. Your purpose and intent for us cannot be thwarted by poor decisions of others or by abrupt changes in life. We will treasure Your sustaining grace even when we would prefer Your delivering grace. You always know what we need to complete the missionary journey You have laid out for us.*

*Today my faith and hope both rise by the power of Your Word and Spirit. Nothing can stop Your kingdom coming and Your will being done on earth as it is Heaven.*

*In Jesus' name,*
*Amen*

---

Thank you for walking with me through Acts 27. If you are currently in a storm, I pray you hear and trust God's sustaining grace. I join with you in turning from fear to faith so we can witness God's goodness to others.

God bless,

Jim

# 52 | A *WALK* THROUGH ACTS 28

In our travels my family and I have received several gift baskets. An early fond memory of a gift basket came from a dear family friend, Nancy Norris. Our four children were already fastened in their seats for the annual pilgrimage to visit family when she brought the goodie bags for the kids. She knew they would enjoy the trip if they had a few extra snacks, coloring books, and other trinkets to keep them occupied. Nancy's gift blessed Sherri and me even more than it did the kids! We will never forget the thoughtfulness expressed in that moment. The bags represent a lifetime of love for our children.

On a couple of occasions I told churches hosting Sherri and me that they had given us a MOAB—Mother of All Bags. Those bags could sustain small villages through a seven-year drought! Sometimes church administrators send an information request sheet to see what we like to drink and our favorite snacks. Frequently the gift bag contains fun things (at least fun for a professor-emeritus person like me) such as paper, pens, and back-up battery for a cell phone. One January a church included leather dress gloves to get me through a few bitter days in northern Ohio. Those gloves still have a place in my winter coat pocket. Gift baskets, regardless of the size, contents, or value, make the receiver feel welcome.

Those gift baskets serve a far different purpose than the ones the Academy of Motion Pictures Arts and Science Oscar acting and directing nominees receive before the awards show each year. In 2016, the last year the sponsoring company published the price tag, the bag weighed in at $232,000 worth of swag. The list ranged from $6 Chapstick to a couple of trips worth about $55,000 each. Donors hoped the entertainment elite would leverage some endorsement their way for the free stuff.

A walk through Acts 28 highlights missionary living in receiving and giving hospitality. The ancient world placed a higher value on hospitality as a functional part of life than what I am likely to ever experience. In many places in Scripture we read of the call to care for strangers as well as examples of doing so. The dangerous nature of travel, limited resources, absence of a "hospitality" industry such as hotels and eating places, migration patterns, and many other factors contributed to the development of hospitality.

Hospitality had its risks then as it does now, but the risk could last a lifetime. Jesus told a prayer illustration of pending shame if the host could not get food for the late-night guest (Luke 11:5–8). The host would rather have an angry neighbor than the shame of being inhospitable. Ancient hospitality lasted for a lifetime. Hospitality went beyond welcoming a guest into the home, washing weary feet, providing a meal and bed, and sharing life stories to exchanging identifying tokens to offer proof of the relationship to others.

Perhaps the modern military challenge coin comes close to this exchange. The token commemorates a significant event or relationship, serves as a reminder of the relationship, and provides a sign to others who may see it. Some ancient families handed the tokens to the next generation to continue the link for many years to come. This kind of hospitality goes far beyond offering a drink of water and a "Y'all come back now" wave.

Paul received hospitality from pagans on Malta after the shipwreck. Luke commented on their "unusual kindness" for the weary, water-logged refugees crawling their way up the rocky beach. As Paul returned the hospitality by assisting in building the fire, a deadly viper latched onto him. Local theology concluded Paul must have been a very wicked man and the god of Justice worked to finish the little man's destruction. Theologies quickly changed to ascribe Paul divinity status when the snake had no impact on his stick-gathering activities. Missionary Paul served as a good houseguest by healing sick people for three months.

Luke does not recount one baptism or Holy Spirit outpouring. I have heard people say Paul failed on Mars Hill because only a few believed. They suggest he should have preached from the Old Testament like he did in synagogues even though the audience had no awareness of the Bible. In this case the healing demonstrated God's power and desire to restore all things, yet no one accepted the truth. Paul modeled being a witnessing guest even when people continued in their pagan ways.

The journey to Rome included hospitality at several points. They stayed with saints along the way. Another group of disciples made the forty-mile trip from Rome to accompany him the rest of the way to his divinely appointed destination. Luke carefully informed his readers that Paul took courage from these encounters. God's work frequently happens in these moments of hospitality.

Thanksgiving and courage result. God is glorified. The Kingdom comes.

Luke ended the book with hospitality. He started the book with disciples welcoming the Holy Spirit after a ten-day wait; decades later the church was living out this hospitality lifestyle. Paul welcomed his enemies as well as friends to his place of house arrest. Hospitality provided the chance to proclaim the kingdom of God and teach "about the Lord Jesus Christ with all boldness and without hindrance" (Acts 28:31, ESV). Chains and guards could not stop hospitable witness. Paul probably had to continue to work his tent-making craft or spend an inheritance to support himself, his team, and his visitors during this time. He did it with joy. The God who welcomed him structured the apostle's life around welcoming others.

Paul's commitment to hospitable witness calls me to pray.

---

*Dear Lord,*

*You always work to restore relationships through hospitality. Your life modeled welcoming those who usually experienced rejection. By letting a woman at a well serve You water, she became an early evangelist in Samaria. You call disciples to practice giving and receiving hospitality as a mark of being like You.*

*Forgive me of thinking people will know You through words of reconciliation without the accompanying deeds of reconciliation. Please forgive me for thinking welcoming others is a failure if they do not choose to be baptized or receive the Holy Spirit after the conversation, cup of coffee, or act of service.*

*I want to be like You and Uncle Paul. I want to give and receive hospitality in a way that witnesses to Your kingdom coming and Your will being done.*

*In Jesus' name,*
*Amen*

---

Thank you for walking with me through this last chapter of Acts. As always Luke calls us to witness the Kingdom in whatever condition we find ourselves. I trust the Master will fill your mind, heart, and hands with the resources to share with others in this season of your life.

God bless,

Jim